Teaching as Inquiry, with a Focus on Priority Learners

Teaching as Inquiry, with a Focus on Priority Learners

Lindsey Conner

In association with Lesley Brown, Judith Bennetts, Sabina Cleary, Rachael Dixon, Margaret Leamy, Ross Palmer and Megan Taylor

NZCER PRESS
New Zealand Council for Educational Research
PO Box 3237
Wellington
New Zealand

© Lindsey Conner, 2015

ISBN 978-1-927231-71-5

This book is not a photocopiable master.
No part of the publication may be copied, stored or communicated in any form by any means (paper or digital), including recording or storing in an electronic retrieval system, without the written permission of the publisher.
Education institutions that hold a current licence with Copyright Licensing New Zealand may copy from this book in strict accordance with the terms of the CLNZ Licence.

A catalogue record for this book is available from the National Library of New Zealand.

Designed by Smartwork Creative Ltd

Cover art: *Mark II* by Lesley Brown.

Contents

Foreword	vii
Acknowledgements	ix
Executive summary	x

Chapter 1: Introduction

What is teaching as inquiry?	1
The importance of addressing the needs of priority learners	9
The importance of school leadership	12
Secondary Student Achievement project	15

Chapter 2: Developing the TAI process

Identifying students' needs	19
Being intentional by focusing on four to five students	21
Focusing on pedagogical changes	24
Narratives as support for inquiry	26
Feedback loops for evaluating TAI	28
Summary	30

Chapter 3: Case studies

Characteristics of the case study schools	32
Sorting out what makes a difference	34
School A	36
School B	49
School C	62
Summary	77

Chapter 4: Influences on pedagogical development

The role of the facilitators	80
Being willing to make changes, and being flexible	84
Developing and using feedback loops	86
Keeping perspective	86
Summary	89

Chapter 5: Developing a learning community

Supporting the team	91
Incremental versus large-scale change	93
Changes related to literacy	95
Changes to assessment practices	96
Changes related to culturally responsive teaching	97
Integrating changes with existing initiatives in a community of learning	100
Summary	102

Chapter: 6 Key findings
    Key enablers for priority learners   105
    Key enablers for teachers and middle learners   106
    Key enablers for professional learning communities   109
    Summary   114

Chapter 7: Recommendations for enhancing the implementation of TAI
    1. What have we learned from this project?   116
    2. Given the benefits of TAI, what are the next steps for enhancing actions so that TAI is more sustainable?   123
    3. How can leaders support effective continued professional learning?   124
    4. How can we use TAI more effectively to address equity issues?   127

Conclusion   127

References   129

Biographical information   133

Index   134

Foreword

Recently professional learning and development has turned a corner. Teachers as leaders of learning are realising that they can be agents of change within their classrooms by focusing on quite specific teaching changes to improve outcomes for their learners. Their moral imperative is clear: they want to improve the life chances of their students.

There have been publications that have called for change in professional learning approaches, and specifically for teachers to use teaching as inquiry (TAI). This volume addresses the question of how teachers might manage TAI as part of their everyday work, and how they can be supported to make a difference, especially for *priority learners*.

The Secondary Student Achievement project was a specific PLD intervention in secondary schools throughout New Zealand to enable continuous professional learning. In this intervention, subject-specific facilitators supported teachers to make changes to their teaching and to observe and evaluate changes for four to five learners. The research project that was associated with this intervention sought appreciative examples of where TAI was working well in three case study schools. The success story examples, interviews and Ministry reports from case study schools enabled us to identify patterns that made success more likely.

The teachers in the project were undertaking TAI that focused specifically on four to five priority learners. We discuss the importance and moral imperative to focus on priority learners like this. The idea is that what works to improve the outcomes for priority learners also works for other learners. This is not to say that individual differences were not valued: as part of the process, teachers were using student-centred evidence to inform their next steps in planning—in other words, their planning was based on information they received from their students about progress.

This book is designed to provide examples of implementing change through TAI in schools. Although it focuses on secondary schooling in New Zealand, the professional learning approach could be applied to all other education sectors and is relevant to education systems beyond

New Zealand. Also, the processes of undertaking TAI, the enablers and the constraints, are potentially transferrable between disciplines. This means the professional learning and development processes can be applied to multiple curriculum areas and schools for a range of improvement initiatives.

This book is likely to be of interest to all senior leaders and school teachers because it provides insights into improving teaching and learning in the simultaneous pursuit of equity and quality. Teachers and researchers setting up professional learning and development using TAI will find the process and examples within this book useful.

We have enjoyed learning about how teachers are approaching the needs of their students with curiosity and a sense of openness, and a willingness to make on-going changes. We hope that you will experience the satisfaction that comes from undertaking such important work together with your colleagues.

Lindsey Conner

Acknowledgements

We would like to thank all the students, teachers and school leaders who participated in the Secondary Student Achievement project with Te Tapuae o Rehua consortium for their willingness to open their doors and share their experiences, insights and materials to support these case study descriptions.

This book is also a result of the collaborative efforts of the facilitation team, without whom the project would not have been implemented. Our thanks to everyone in the consortium, and especially to those who worked with teachers to enable them to write their success stories.

Executive summary

This book is about how teachers can use teaching as inquiry (TAI) to continuously improve teaching and learning. It provides teachers and researchers with background and case study examples of what made a difference, especially for priority learners in schools. It is based on the experiences of school leaders, facilitators, teachers and students during the implementation of the Secondary Student Achievement project, funded by the New Zealand Ministry of Education over a 3-year period.

TAI was introduced to the teachers in this project as a frame of reference for considering changes to pedagogy to support the aspirations of *The New Zealand Curriculum* (Ministry of Education, 2007, p. 35). The professional learning and development (PLD) contract funded facilitators to work with middle leaders and teachers with the specific agenda to raise achievement among priority learners. Teachers re-examined their curriculum and teaching practices so that they were able to progress the achievement of Māori and Pasifika students, students with special education needs, students from low socioeconomic backgrounds, and English-language learners (ELLs).

Three school-wide case studies are presented in this book to provide some specific examples of how they (leaders and teachers) implemented TAI and the next steps as they see them. The contextual nuances of each school, each class and each learning situation indicate how the process of TAI can be applied to multiple contexts. These examples also indicate how whole-school support for TAI through the spirit of continuous improvement helped to build a sense of learning together. They also indicate that changing the culture of a school to one of continuous improvement is a collective responsibility of all within the school community: leaders (mana whakatipu), teachers (kaiako) and learners (ākonga) together.

Developing a 'learning together' culture was very important for all three schools. In general, the teachers who participated actively in TAI in these schools gained confidence and competence, linked to their perception that there was a professional environment or ethos within the school that supported them to undertake TAI. It is fair to say that the teachers' capabilities and capacities to mentor others to reflect and refine practice across the schools are still emerging. More opportunities to extend professional learning by sharing practices that engage Pasifika and Māori students are likely to enhance and spread good practice in the future. The schools are moving towards working with other schools and making use of in-depth cluster expertise.

The case study schools were chosen to indicate examples of where TAI was successful. The case studies are structured according to progress and success factors at multiple levels: the whole school, the department or faculty, and the individual teachers. The core elements for longer-term sustainability are also considered, such as:

- how TAI has become embedded as part of the school culture, including building teachers' capability and capacity to mentor others
- how schools have developed coherence throughout their schools so that individual teachers' changes and departmental or group initiatives contribute to their common and agreed goals.

In general, some of the teachers in the case study schools have embraced the concept of TAI very well. The discussion presents the enablers and considerations when implementing targeted TAI.

Within the case study schools, teachers' and facilitators' success stories indicated how TAI led to changes in curriculum focus, pedagogy and assessment practices. These included the formative processes that build student capabilities, as well as reconsiderations of the types of formative tasks, learning and feedback or feed-forward that students need in order to progress. The schools are monitoring shifts in student outcomes, especially shifts for their targeted four to five priority learners. The case studies were developed from interviews, observations, facilitator reports, Education Review Office (ERO) reports, and success stories of practice-based interventions alongside student achievement data.

The key findings are considered in terms of the longer-term sustainability of practices for enabling on-going improvement. Some of the teachers in the case study schools have embraced the concept of TAI very well and are considering how they can mentor and lead others. Within the case studies, we identified the enablers and challenges for making changes to teaching and how these changes contributed to the enhancement of students' outcomes, especially for priority learners.

Chapter 1: Introduction

What is teaching as inquiry?

The teaching as inquiry (TAI) approaches described in this book are closely connected with the purpose of changing the life chances of young people. TAI has, at its core, the purpose of redressing inequity while simultaneously enhancing the quality of teaching and learning. It is based on previous findings that indicate the important role that curious leaders and teachers play in making a difference for their learners.

TAI is an approach to teaching—not an add-on or something extra that teachers are expected to do. When implemented as part of teaching, it supports teachers to be more effective in planning, teaching and reflecting on what they do, because it requires a specific focus or decisions and actions (see Figure 1). TAI is more of a mindset towards teaching, where students' needs are central and refinements to teaching are continuous.

Educators with inquiry mindsets are continuously searching for refinements to their practice and are comfortable with the fact that there will inevitably be a range of outcomes in response to their efforts. Rather than searching for *solutions*, inquiring teachers continuously seek *improvements*, knowing that there are always alternative ways of doing things. They sidestep the idea that "I already do that", because they know there are always other approaches and they are concerned about their learners' progress. This has been recognised in the New Zealand education system for some time, and is reflected in the curriculum documents and has been the subject of ERO evaluations (ERO, 2010, 2012).

The New Zealand Curriculum states that the process for TAI involves teachers monitoring and reflecting critically on the impact of their decisions on student learning (Ministry of Education, 2007, p. 35). The approach taken to TAI in this project was more specific than the curriculum implies: although TAI was introduced to the teachers as a frame of reference for considering changes to pedagogy to support the aspirations of *The New Zealand Curriculum*, teachers were asked to specifically focus on the needs of four to five priority learners in order to manage and monitor the effects of the changes they made more effectively.

Figure 1: Teaching as inquiry in action

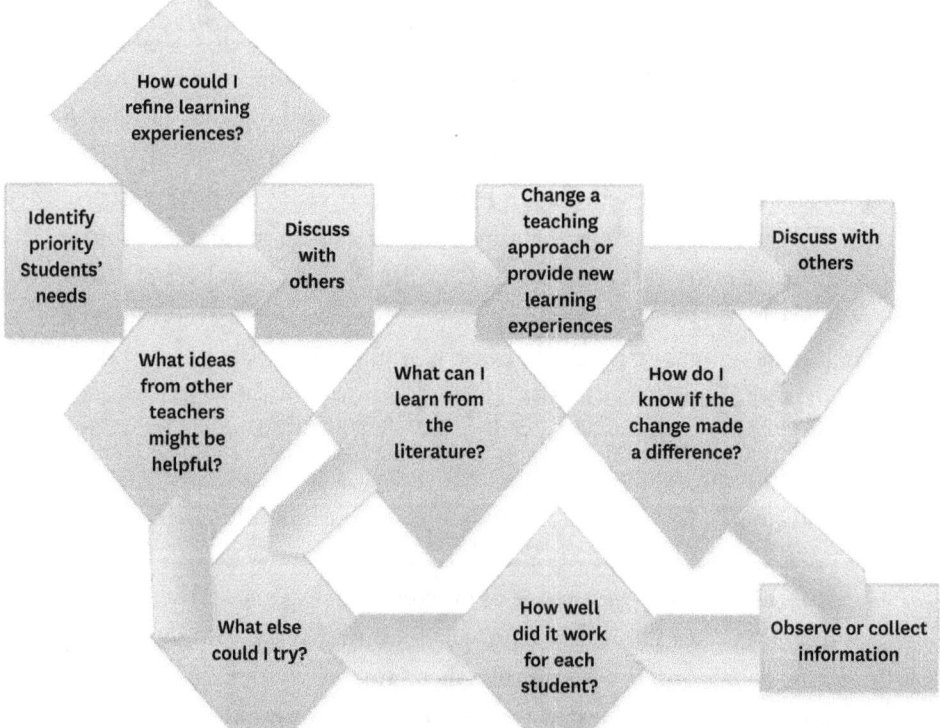

Visually, the process of TAI for priority learners is represented in Figure 1. This representation differs from previous diagrams of TAI (Halbert & Kaser, 2013; Ministry of Education, 2007; Timperley, 2011b) in that it promotes decision making *and* action as core elements in the ongoing cyclical process in relation to priority learners. This is because the evaluation of TAI undertaken by ERO (2012) indicated that where inquiry is working well, all phases of the inquiry cycle are occurring.

Identifying student needs is only the first—and probably the easiest—step in TAI as teachers learn to use a range of classroom diagnostic and formative tools. The ERO evaluation discussed how teachers and leaders were stronger at identifying the needs of students than they were at identifying, planning and taking action, and evaluating changes in learning. The report stated that there was a need for leaders and teachers to:

1. draw on a wider range of research and/or effective practice when they designed programmes and interventions for learners
2. make better use of evidence when they evaluated outcomes for learners and the programmes and initiatives they had put in place
3. use the information they had about students' learning strengths and needs to design appropriate professional learning and development opportunities for teachers. (ERO, 2012, p. 1)

The ERO report also discussed how disappointing it was to see how the support in schools for TAI had declined in some of the schools they evaluated between 2009 and 2011. This may have been because there was an assumption that teachers would drive their own TAI but this was not necessarily the case. This assumption underpins why the Secondary Student Achievement project was supported by the Ministry, which recognised that teachers needed ongoing support to develop the skills and implement complete cycles of TAI. Leaders in schools did not necessarily have experience with TAI, nor did they know what teachers needed to sustain them longer term. Therefore expert subject facilitators (advisers) provided guidance at multiple levels to seed ideas about changes in teaching and to sustain teachers' focus on the evaluation of their efforts.

In the Secondary Student Achievement project, TAI places the students' needs as the starting point (Figure 1). In this project the facilitators worked with the teachers and middle leaders on all of the diamonds in Figure 1. The idea is to start with observations or identify what students need, then develop your own inquiry by asking questions directly related to making changes to teaching, based on the needs of the learners. Rather than recycling generalised solutions, teachers figure out how they can make a difference for their priority learners. There will be a range of ways to know if their changes in teaching have made a difference, by observing student behaviour or by collecting examples of student work.

Teachers, as participants in TAI, are continuously curious about how they know they have made a difference. They also seek information—from significant other people (including facilitators and colleagues), the literature, and other sources of inspiration. They then take action by making a change in a teaching approach. Thus there are cycles of observation and evidence of outcomes, and these are linked to continuous efforts to refine approaches to teaching.

Through our observations in this project we are convinced that individual teachers can undertake TAI by themselves and make a difference for their students. However, there is much more educational 'lift' when teachers have input on possible actions or are guided. Therefore we wanted to consider how individual teachers and supports within a school-wide implementation of TAI enabled school-wide change, since schools as educational entities are very keen to progress how, as a school, they are making a difference. School-wide educational lift will be faster and potentially more effective when teachers share their development as part of the professional learning environment within a school (Timperley, 2011b).

Also, it seems important to support specific subjects with targeted facilitation, and to support teachers with context-relevant advice so that they become familiar with TAI processes. The value of developing TAI initially with middle leaders should not be underestimated. This is because when middle leaders 'get it', and understand TAI in more depth, they are more likely to be able to support other teachers. The facilitation support should therefore relate to the specific knowledge and experience of the teachers involved. In this project, the facilitators were very aware of the way their subject knowledge and professional knowledge could support teachers and middle leaders to grow professionally. As one middle leader in a rural school stated:

> I feel that a can-do attitude has been fostered through quality professional dialogue, a narrow and deep focus on target students and continued reflection around these individuals. Tools and resources have been provided to assist the achievement of this group and I have found that although the target is a small group, the wider cohort all gain the benefits of the project and assistance I am being offered. (School leader)

The subject-specialist facilitators were pivotal in initiating and supporting the whole TAI process (Figure 1). (There is a more detailed discussion of this in Chapters 5 and 6.) While the role of the subject specialist facilitators was to guide and support teachers' professional learning, essentially they:

- helped teachers to identify what their priority students' needs were
- as a consequence, helped the teachers to identify their own professional needs, provided resources to support specific pedagogical interventions, and enabled the teachers to reflect on how they knew whether the intervention had made a difference
- invited the teachers to provide success stories.

An example of a teacher's success story shows how she developed aspects of the TAI cycle with the assistance of her facilitator.

Success story: Geography class

At the beginning of 2013, and after I pre-tested my geography Level 3 class, I realised that I needed to focus on a target group of six students: three Māori and three Pākehā, three females and three males. My subject facilitator observed me each term and conducted interviews with my target students. Based on students' weaknesses of basic geography mapping, graphing, concept description skills and history paragraph and essay-writing skills, I offered scaffolding for planning, used graphic organisers, established 'peer panel' marking as a daily lesson practice, gave lots of homework and modelled answers. As a result my target group built core geography skills, conceptual understanding, and I kept differentiating tasks, as my facilitator suggested, to help the new-to-the-subject students. The outcome was that four of my target students gained an Achieved grade in the first internal achievement standard, one gained Merit and one Excellence; also they gained two Achieved and one Achieved with Merit grade in the first mock examination.

The model in Figure 1 is open ended in that any one of multiple aspects of teaching and learning could be chosen as a focus. Subject specialists were able to provide suggestions for what teachers could focus on for their TAI, but this had to be based on students' needs. There could be multiple ideas to address the needs of priority learners. Fullan (2007) uses the term "simplexity" to describe the fact that we want better student outcomes but achieved in the most effective way possible. What has been applied in one context and its outcomes can inform another context, but the students in one setting will be different and their backgrounds will be different to those in another setting. Therefore, teacher actions must be student and context based. We recognised this at the outset and therefore sought case studies to illustrate how teachers addressed these issues in their particular contexts.

Interestingly, the teachers discovered that while they can learn good ideas from their own interventions and from others, transfer of specific interventions does not always work. Some of the teachers were confronted with their assumption that what worked in one context should work in another. This applied especially when they had experienced success related to the changes they made in the 1st year of implementation. As a consequence, some teachers had to rethink the application of their teaching approaches in the 2nd year in relation to the specific needs of their current students.

It seems that very few studies have investigated the specific links between changes in teaching and consequent changes to student outcomes (Desimone, 2009; Timperley, Wilson, Barrar, & Fung, 2007). This is because establishing direct causal links between teacher and student learning is problematic since it downplays the complexities inherent within teacher and student learning. There are not necessarily repeatable causes and effects related to the specific changes teachers make: often changes are context dependent and therefore not transferable. This is understandable when student needs come first, since student needs (even for the same student) are highly likely to vary in different learning contexts. However, the process of TAI can be used in any teaching or learning situation.

Other studies on the PLD of teachers have shown that where teachers were able to reflect, choose an area for their own development (Turvey, 2013), access new ideas and share their experiences through a TAI process, their growth, wellbeing and success were enhanced (Hargreaves, 1994; Muijs, Day, Harris, & Lindsay, 2004). In their introduction, Halbert and Kaser (2012, p. 4) describe TAI as being flexible and tailored to learners' needs:

> Inquiry is not about the pursuit of the perfect question or the next exciting project. It is about being open to new learning and taking informed action. Innovation is not about sprinkling initiatives like pixie dust, hoping they will stick nor is it about what is new and groovy. Innovation is about recognising that old forms are not working for all learners, identifying what the key needs of our learners are, and then creating new forms based on knowledge about what does work.

Evaluating professional learning in terms of the multiple impacts of the changes at different levels within a school (and for a wider professional learning project) is worthy of serious attention (Muijs et al., 2004). There are likely to be complex ways of improving both equity and quality (Blankstein & Noguera, 2015) of student outcomes that need to be figured out, with the context taken into account. Therefore this study considered cases and vignettes of longer-term changes in teachers' thinking and actions, alongside changes in the way subject specialist facilitators and schools were enabling professional learning related to improving priority students' learning.

What is becoming apparent from this project, and the literature, is that teachers who have changed their pedagogies in response to the needs of their students, and who have observed positive student changes as a consequence of these changes to teaching, consider this as success that propels them to consider their next iteration of change. In this way, teacher agency can be developed (Conner, 2013; Turvey, 2013). Although improving student outcomes is the primary motivation for teachers, teacher change through TAI as professional learning requires deep intellectual and emotional investments from teachers, and it takes time (Timperley, 2011b). In particular, teachers need to have identified specific teaching problems or issues related to student learning that drive their "need to know" (Timperley, 2011a). Teachers will have different previous experiences and capabilities related to evidence-informed and evidence-generating practices. This means different teachers may need different levels of support for different stages of the TAI process (Figure 1).

Professional learning should benefit individuals, groups or schools to enhance the quality of educational outcomes (Day, 1999). There is a moral imperative to do so. Renewing and extending teacher knowledge, skills and thinking can occur through individual or collaborative efforts that are designed to implement approaches for enhancing students' learning experiences. For TAI to be effective it has to be a collaborative effort between the "student, teacher and organization" (Timperley et al., 2007, p. xiii). Therefore, any evaluation of TAI must take account of both the direct and indirect effects of teacher changes on different stakeholders (Muijs et al., 2004). One of the indirect effects targeted in this project was the benefits to the department or school (as well as benefits to the teachers and students), particularly how the teachers' inquiry processes and successes contributed to the changing culture of teaching in each school.

What is accepted as usual practice and how teacher learning and change are prioritised within a school—contributes to the school culture. Effective professional development occurs when school structures and school culture support the changes that are needed. This requires developing feedback loops for teachers and leaders to work out what teachers need to support their on-going inquiries. There may also need to be changes to school structures and developmental initiatives to support groups of staff.

A previous meta-study (Timperley et al., 2007) identified 97 research projects that linked teacher professional development to changes in student outcomes. Despite this number, few studies provided detail and adequate reporting of specific PLD and its consequent outcomes for priority learners.

The importance of addressing the needs of priority learners

Since the 1980s some education systems have become less equitable in terms of access to education that can enable learners from diverse backgrounds to succeed. This is a worldwide issue that needs to be addressed urgently. Blankstein and Noguera (2015, p. 7) insist that "demography need not determine destiny, and a child's race and class *can* be decoupled from how well they will do in school or college".

Of prime interest is how (and whether) teachers and schools consider that all students have latent talents that can be enhanced. How educators enable these talents to shine should be the focus of our attention. This will no doubt involve prioritising our energy and focus, as well as our resources. As Blankstein and Noguera (2015) show, striving for success for our most disadvantaged students also requires courageous leadership and commitment to ensuring that every child gets what he or she needs to succeed. They indicate that we have to address the fact that some children are denied the opportunity to have their talents developed because their families do not have the resources (time, knowledge, skills and/or money) to invest in them. TAI can help to identify what students need, and potentially identify steps to redress inequity.

The diversity of students in the New Zealand education system is one of its strengths. We are very fortunate to have a school curriculum that supports diverse approaches and celebrates the fact that teachers can and should focus on the needs of their individual learners (Ministry of Education, 2007). However, this is somewhat daunting when faced with trying to do so for up to 30 students in a class.

There is general guidance for how teachers might work with individual differences, such as *Tātaiako* (New Zealand Teachers Council, 2010a), the *Pasifika Education Plan* (Ministry of Education, 2012b) and *Ka Hikitia—Accelerating Success 2013-2017* (Ministry of Education, 2012a) and its predecessor plan, which have supported school leaders and facilitators to develop and refine teachers' understanding of cultural competence. However, there is still much work to be done so that teachers can understand and identify needs, and be responsive to diverse identities, languages and cultures.

To move this forward, facilitators in this project have supported teachers to make sense of what the five cultural competencies (New Zealand Teachers Council, 2012a) mean for them within their teaching context and to meaningfully integrate the principles into their teaching practice. School leaders are also considering how communication can be more culturally appropriate, how visual components in and around the school reflect a sense of place and belonging, and how relationships among staff and between staff and students can support cultural aspirations. A focus on cultural dimensions at a whole-school level will support school lift in engagement and achievement (Macfarlane, 2004).

The Case for System-wide Improvement (Ministry of Education, 2012c) showed that the demographics of groups in the New Zealand population are changing. In the last census over half (53 percent) of Māori were under 25 years of age, compared with just over a third (36 percent) of the total population. These young people are our future citizens, and we need to prepare them adequately to live meaningful lives. Our future societal development depends on them. The knowledge, skills and competencies they can develop are important not only to them and their communities, but also to the nation.

Currently the general observation that students attending low socioeconomic status schools have lower overall achievement rates indicates that meritocracy is something of a false premise. While the New Zealand National Certificate of Educational Achievement (NCEA)[1] achievement standards provide a framework for inclusion, the achievement rates suggest otherwise. Individual talent and tenacity do not necessarily overcome social obstacles that might avert success.

Also, lower school retention rates for Māori students mean they are under-represented in the later years of schooling and are more likely to leave with fewer school qualifications. There are social reasons for these outcomes (Bishop & Glynn, 1999). Sadly, as much as we might have hoped the developments in NCEA would have moved the education system in New Zealand forward, it tends to reinforce inequity prematurely or inaccurately, making judgments about the ability of children that may actually be exacerbating the achievement gap (Haque, 2014).

---

1 The National Certificate of Educational Achievement is New Zealand's school exit qualification, with Level 1, 2, and 3 certificates corresponding broadly to the final three years of secondary school.

Hargreaves (2015) strongly stated this in relation to what teachers in the USA must do, but these sentiments could equally apply to New Zealand teachers and educators more widely:

> To increase the human capital of our students, we must invest in the professional capital of our teachers … America must communicate strong and positive messages about the value of teachers and teaching and also back them up by articulating a compelling vision for America's students and their schools, by improving the working conditions for teachers—especially teachers' opportunities to collaborate with each other—and by according more flexibility to teachers to design curriculum and develop pedagogical expertise together. (Hargreaves, 2015, p. 285)

This statement could equally be applied to the New Zealand education system. Recently the Hechinger Report (Bailey, 2014) indicated that providing teachers with more time to collaborate yields better outcomes than extending the learning time for students who are not achieving well. It also indicated that when teachers take the time to get to know their students, they are more likely to be able to attend to the students' mental health and wellbeing, particularly if they are not overwhelmed with implementing multiple initiatives simultaneously.

The evidence from our project indicates that teachers who prioritise their focus on developing students' sub-skills, and identify appropriate responses and actions that they as teachers can take, become more confident as teachers. This aligns with helping and guiding students to be more actively involved in self-assessing and directing their own learning in what Hipkins (2015, p. viii) regards as "students' active involvement in a range of assessment practices." Hipkins indicates that it is very important to grow "student assessment capability", because students develop their understanding of the requirements of assessments better and therefore have more capability to monitor their approaches to learning. Teachers can help to guide students on what to focus on, depending on the specific requirements of assessments and students' assessment of their own capabilities.

We have observed teachers who have been supported to develop their teaching through small changes and interventions. Examples of some of the pedagogical shifts are provided in Chapters 2 and 3. Many of the teachers in our project schools were seriously and continuously embracing pedagogy for meeting the specific needs of their focus learners. They are finding that tracking the learning of four to five learners keeps the more detailed approach to using evidence of learning for priority students—and responding to this evidence—manageable.

To varying extents all of the leaders in the three case study schools employed the idea that TAI could make a difference for priority learners. We observed in School C (see Chapter 3) how the moral imperative was more clearly a driver behind the decisions the principal made. Potentially this in itself helped drive the teachers at this school to engage with TAI purposefully, and consequently there were more shifts in teaching practices and positive effects on student outcomes. School-wide and system-wide lift will occur when the moral imperative to use TAI for improving outcomes for priority learners is embraced. Leaders have a clear role in articulating this and being relentless in making it clear.

The importance of school leadership

If we take the moral imperative above seriously, then the drive for equity within schools requires committed and well-organised leadership. Hargreaves (2015, p. 286) writes that "equity is about uplift as an end". This may require leaders to inspire their teams through their own personal courage and tenacity to motivate those around them. There should be a leadership focus on enabling teams to succeed, rather than a focus on compliance or the performance management of individuals.

The importance of the involvement of school leaders in whole-school initiatives seems obvious. Leaders matter (Robinson, Hohepa, & Lloyd, 2009) because they create and maintain the environment and can use the systems within the school to support implementation and acceptance as 'part of what we do here'. They can provide resources and create structures and procedures that can support teachers to make a difference. However, not all school leaders get involved in the specific implementation of an initiative. Often the details are delegated to a senior leader within the school. We have observed across the 47 schools involved in the Secondary Student Achievement project the influence of the principal when they actively monitor progress of implementation of TAI and keep a close eye on actions and ongoing progress in meeting expectations.

A meta-analysis (best evidence synthesis) of effective leadership practices (Robinson et al., 2009) indicated that leadership practices can have a large, very educationally significant effect on student outcomes. Leaders were found to have a more direct influence when they provided both informal and formal opportunities for teacher learning and development. For example, staff in high-performing schools reported that their leaders worked directly with teachers or departmental heads to plan, co-ordinate and evaluate teachers and teaching. Such leaders tended to provide professional evaluations that teachers found useful, and ensured student progress was monitored and assessment results were used to inform the next practices that could improve teaching.

Robinson et al. also found that when leaders are actively involved in professional learning, they are more likely to implement the necessary changes by making adjustments to class organisation, resourcing, and assessment procedures. They become more attuned to the issues of practice and what needs to be changed. If they actively participate in TAI, they are modelling how they value it as a process.

Developing and supporting the effective functioning of professional learning among staff have been shown to support teachers to learn professionally, especially when they are focused on improving student success as a collective (Carnell & Lodge, 2002; Harris, 2002; Timperley, 2011a, 2011b; Wenger, McDermott, & Snyder, 2002). In order to establish and sustain such communities, leaders may need to challenge or change existing school cultures to support collegial discussion about the relationship between teaching and enabling learning. It may also require leaders to remind teachers more than once about the purpose and potential gains for students—the *why* of being involved. Successful and sustainable professional learning communities are associated with a strong sense of collective.

Leadership for learning is more likely when leaders ensure that teachers prioritise student learning, make shifts and changes in their teaching to enable more effective learning, and as a group take collective responsibility and accountability for students' achievement and wellbeing. In an ERO report (2014) the evaluation team found that in schools where the principals were successfully managing change, they were very knowledgeable and skillful, and exhibited the characteristics of powerful leadership. In other words, they were able to identify what their community of learners (students and teachers) needed and were able to take action to support progress.

Effective teacher inquiry is contingent on a strong vision for the purpose and outcomes related to professional learning in schools and how this is linked to improving student outcomes. Where TAI was working well, and in the three schools described in Chapter 3, the leaders of the schools had incorporated TAI into the schools' appraisal processes as a tool and lever for continuous professional learning that all teachers should be engaged in. Initially, in all three schools this was considered by some teachers to be inappropriate. There is still some disquiet in these schools that ongoing progress with professional learning should be decoupled from appraisal. This issue is discussed further in Chapter 5. The importance of school leaders in enabling the vision to be articulated, driving the culture of continuous improvement and shaping how teachers focus on inquiry as part of their continuous professional learning should not be underestimated.

While good teachers reflect on their teaching and routinely make changes associated with identifying the needs of their students, not all teachers do this naturally. They often need to be immersed in a culture where it is acceptable to take risks and reflect on what could be improved. Or they may need to be convinced that undertaking TAI is useful. The leaders in our study also needed to be convinced. A facilitator's success story highlights how a principal led the literacy development of his school.

Success story: Literacy facilitator

Early in term 4 of a school year, as professional learning facilitator in adolescent literacy, I was approached by the literacy leader of a large, urban, integrated boys' school seeking support in developing a school literacy development programme. I subsequently worked with the school for just over 2 years. From my point of view what ensured the programme's continuance and acceptance by pretty much the whole teaching staff was the obvious leadership by the principal. Because he knew intimately how the programme was structured, what the professional learning being undertaken involved and what the specific intentions were for student learning, he was able to promote and support the programme in detailed, practical ways every week.

The teaching staff knew he knew, and were therefore ready to accept his leading them to reflect on and develop their teaching practices with regard to student literacy development.

In this case the principal embraced the vision for improving whole-school leadership and indicated specific strategies for staff to help them focus on literacy as a priority.

He did not discard what teachers had done previously, but rather used the power of reflection to focus on what was needed for future practice. Looking back was a key step to moving forward!

Secondary Student Achievement project

The Secondary Student Achievement Professional Learning and Development contract was funded by the Ministry of Education to enable subject-specific facilitators to support middle teachers to re-examine their curriculum and teaching practices in order to improve outcomes for priority learners. Schools and facilitators from the University of Canterbury and University of Otago, in partnership with Ngā Rūnunga through Te Tapuae o Rehua Ltd[2] worked together to develop TAI. The implementation of TAI project Mau ki te ako (grasping or enhancing learning and teaching), included all learning areas of *the New Zealand Curriculum* but not all learning areas were included in all schools. This project differed from previous PLD in that it required teachers to focus on four to five priority learners only. In this case, priority learners included Māori and Pasifika students, students with special education needs, and students from low socioeconomic backgrounds. This particular form of TAI was implemented in 47 schools across New Zealand and was informed by previous research on TAI (Halbert & Kaser, 2013; Kaser & Halbert, 2014; Timperley, 2011a, 2011b).

The research project that was associated with the implementation of TAI is the subject of this book. It was specifically designed to consider examples of success and to provide rich descriptions of cases. We wanted to develop in-depth examples of cases where we considered patterns that emerged from the leadership, changes to teaching,

---

2 Te Tapuae o Rehua Ltd is the company set up to support the local iwi (tribe), Ngai Tahu, which has supported high school teacher PLD across all learning areas.

facilitation and student outcomes. This research was bound by and utilised ethical practices such as anonymity and confidentiality. Ethical approval was obtained through the University of Canterbury Human Ethics Committee. All participants in the research project were volunteers and there were no incentives to take part nor were they obliged to from the perspective of the school management.

TAI is depicted as spirals of change by Kaser and Halbert (2014), who present a cyclical professional learning approach and refer to ongoing teacher change and learning as spirals. They link the inquiry and professional learning to the question 'What's going on for our learners?' in order to emphasise a learner-centred approach as the focus for PLD, rather than a pedagogical or teacher performance emphasis.

What is becoming apparent in similar studies on TAI (Halbert & Kaser, 2013; Rozenszajn & Yarden, 2014; Timperley, 2011a) is that this type of PLD is customised for individual teachers, whereby a facilitator guides the design and focus of the teacher's inquiry and provides mentoring and background information or pedagogical ideas that appeal to each teacher's unique orientation. In this way, the facilitated TAI approach recognises that there will be diversity in the backgrounds and experiences of the teachers, as much as there is variation in students' needs. This approach supports the development of each teacher's own professional knowledge and skills to enhance them for improved student outcomes.

In this project, subject-specialist secondary facilitators connected with middle teachers to focus on aspects of curriculum design based on student learning progress information, pedagogical change (including the use of ICT), assessment practices, and the inclusion of subject-specific literacy and culturally responsive approaches to teaching and learning. The teachers in this project realised they had to build on the strengths of their past practice—use the present learning information to design the future learning experiences—but also that this was an ongoing process.

In this PLD project we were particularly interested in the processes that enable teachers to develop their inquiry skills and what leadership strategies and school-wide processes support the schools to enable progress with TAI. Professional learning should contribute to the benefit of individuals, groups and schools to enhance the quality of educational outcomes (Day, 1999). Renewing and extending teacher knowledge, skills and thinking can occur through individual or collaborative efforts that are designed to implement approaches for enhancing students' learning experiences (Harris, 2002).

> *"The teachers in this project realised they had to build on the strengths of their past practice—use the present learning information to design the future learning experiences—but also that this was an ongoing process."*

For TAI to be effective, it has to be a collaborative effort between the "student, teacher and organization" (Timperley et al., 2007, p. xiii). Therefore considerations about TAI must take account of both the direct and indirect effects of teacher changes on different stakeholders (Muijs et al., 2004). One of the indirect effects targeted in this project was to include the benefits to the department or school (as well as benefits to the teachers and students), particularly how the teachers' inquiry processes and successes contributed to the changing culture of teaching in each school.

Effective professional development occurs when school structures and school culture support the changes that are needed. Feedback loops to help senior management find out what resources teachers need are very important. Therefore the structures and developmental initiatives at a whole-school level need oversight and leadership to make sure they are supporting the development of groups of staff. School leaders play a crucial role in all aspects of developing a culture of continuous professional learning. As Levin (2010, p. 309) wrote:

> Change strategies are comprehensive with an emphasis not only on professional capacity building and strong leadership, but also on targeted resources and effective engagement of parents and the broader community.

While the cases presented in Chapter 3 indicate specific interventions undertaken by teachers in response to the identified needs of the students in their care, the in-depth examples from three case study schools indicate patterns of experience and contextual nuances that were reflected in the wider project as it progressed in the 47 schools where the project was being implemented. Due to the scope of the project, it was not possible to collect and synthesise the qualitative information from all 47 schools to the same depth as these three case study schools.

Guiding questions

1. How might identifying the needs of four to five learners help you to focus on developing an inquiry project?
2. What kinds of evidence could you use to find out if the changes in your teaching are making a difference to students?
3. Can you give an example of where you have prompted or guided students to think about their own specific learning strengths and needs?
4. What do leaders need to keep in mind when implementing schoolwide TAI?
5. If there were two ideas that you would like to share with other teachers about TAI, what would they be?

Chapter 2: Developing the TAI process

This project was not designed to convince teachers and leaders that TAI is useful. Previous studies have already established this (Halbert & Kaser, 2013; Timperley, 2011a, 2011b). For example, the ERO (2012) evaluation stated:

> There are clear benefits for students and teachers when inquiry happens well. Firstly, students' needs and strengths are responded to quickly and more precisely because teachers have up-to-the-minute information on which to base their teaching decisions. Secondly, the feedback loops that are established when teachers observe, respond and evaluate in 'real time' improve their teaching practices. (p. 2)

In this chapter, aspects of developing the steps in the inquiry process are discussed in more detail. These include identifying students' needs, being intentional by focusing on four to five students, and focusing on pedagogical changes and feedback loops to evaluate progress in student and teacher learning.

Identifying students' needs

Students' needs are the core of the TAI process used in this project (Figure 1, see p. 2), because this aligns the professional learning with the aspirations of *The New Zealand Curriculum* and to meet the individual needs of priority learners in particular. There is a dilemma in focusing on students' needs in terms of individual needs versus small-group or whole-class needs, because in identifying these, the teacher has an obligation to address them when they may not be able to meet all the needs of even a small group of students.

Until recently, teachers in secondary schools have found it difficult to manage the scope of addressing the individual needs of all their students. It is not that teachers don't know how to do this; rather, when they see over 100 students a day it is difficult for them to manage the multiple complexities that identifying and addressing individual students' needs implies. Therefore, part of the role of the facilitators was to help teachers identify and prioritise which learners they would focus on and in which classes. Then teachers needed support to identify what needs their priority learners had, and which needs were most important or could be addressed by making relatively small changes to their teaching approaches.

Many of the students had needs related to developing their written or oral communication skills. The teachers who focused on subject-specific literacy quickly realised that effective process-writing skills were very important for achieving higher grades in NCEA achievement standards. This is because discriminating skills when working with a range of sources of information, and linking ideas and being able to communicate key ideas and discuss concepts from multiple points of view, is valued in many learning area assessment tasks. For example, one head of department (HOD) for English found that her priority students needed more structured examples to develop their ideas in their written work. The facilitator and the teacher discussed possible interventions that could be implemented with the whole class to support this and chose to use the TEXAS structure for paragraphs in literary essays.[1] While the students were already familiar with the term 'TEXAS', they were not yet able to develop TEXAS paragraphs independently and consistently write well. Together the facilitator and the teacher developed learning intentions and success criteria to help the students to develop their understanding of structuring paragraphs.

As part of this intervention, students analysed and critiqued sample paragraphs in relation to the TEXAS structure, working individually

---

[1] The TEXAS acronym stands for topic sentence, explanation, example, analysis, summary. This is a common structure used in many New Zealand secondary schools and one that students can use for many types of writing.

and in small groups. When they were next provided with a written assessment, the students and the teacher saw a noticeable improvement in their writing structures. She made the following comment in relation to this:

> The students did reasonably in the exams but the outstanding thing was that all the attempted essays were well-structured. When I asked them [the students] why they thought this was so they said it was the work on TEXAS paragraphs alongside of the work we had done on structure. (HOD English)

Through discussion, the teacher and facilitator together had changed her approach to teaching process writing, and this seemed to improve the structure of students' paragraph writing. More examples of these sorts of changes are provided later in this book.

Being intentional by focusing on four to five students

Simply maintaining the status quo was not acceptable to the teachers in these schools. They knew that the huge disparities for priority learners in the New Zealand education system need to be addressed and that doing more of the same was not likely to make a difference. Therefore they had to change something in their practice.

There was a tension among the leaders and facilitators, who knew that it was advisable to introduce innovations that were informed by previous experience, but also knew that creativity can lead to new ideas or pockets of innovation that have not been previously considered. Therefore, as part of the professional learning, teachers and facilitators sought external research, documents and articles from journals to support professional learning. These documents provided teachers with some information and examples about inquiry approaches. Keeping TAI manageable implied they had to focus on four to five learners only and on what these specific students needed, otherwise they would not be directly aligning their changes to the purpose of improving outcomes for their priority learners. This sets this inquiry process apart from previous studies (e.g. Kaser & Talbert, 2014; Timperley, 2011b).

> *"Relatively early on in the first year, whole-school approaches or emphases were disbanded in the three case study schools."*

For this reason, although teachers shared their outcomes as part of professional learning groups (PLGs), relatively early on in the first year whole-school approaches or emphases were disbanded in the three case study schools in our project. Instead, there was a shift to developing overarching goals of what was to be achieved, and teachers were given the freedom to choose how they would address the specific needs of their priority learners. This is also somewhat different from previous Ministry of Education initiatives, such as Te Kotahitanga and some of the Building on Success interventions, which, while also emphasising the importance of raising Māori achievement, have tended to be more prescriptive in their approaches to changes to teaching.

Consequently, individual teachers (who were supported by a facilitator) considered their professional learning needs based on their focus students' needs. This led to pockets of innovation in teaching. For example, some of the leaders of these schools discussed how they started out by providing guidelines for staff with specific boxes to be filled in, in the spirit of guiding staff and getting them started. However, staff in one case study school insisted that this was not working for them, so this whole-school approach was replaced by a more student-centred one that focused on what mattered for the focus students. As a result, this gave teachers a lot more choice, freedom and agency to create their own (and supported) solutions, which they tried out and evaluated.

The success story of a health teacher indicated that substantial gains in achievement were made when the teacher focused on students' strengths and needs. Her class was small and she knew the students well, having taught them (and having focused on them for her inquiry) the previous year, so she selected three Māori girls and one boy for her focused inquiry. Based on her prior knowledge of these students' achievement, she identified that these students were all at risk of Not Achieving in Year 12 health NCEA for a range of reasons.

The facilitator's success story substantiated the teacher's claims. Both stories provided insight into how the health teacher used a range of tools as evidence sources to establish the focus students' learning strengths, needs and goals. Support from the facilitator included ideas for collecting student voice, where the teacher had conversations with the students about their NCEA achievement in relation to their records from the previous year. On the basis of this information two students needed:

- academic mentoring (goal setting, reflections on progress and learning)
- specific literacy-based supports.

> "She appreciated the importance of digging deeper to find out more about students' strengths and needs in order to respond accordingly."

The teacher and facilitator discussed what the teacher currently did in relation to these aspects. Then the teacher indicated that one of her strengths as a teacher was the positive learning relationship she had with her students and her ability to act as a mentor for them. She acknowledged that she had learnt a lot about literacy from her inquiry during the previous year, but she wanted to deepen her skills and understanding about using a range of literacy tools to support the students better.

The facilitator guided the teacher by providing a number of professional readings relating to literacy in health contexts that could be used with her Year 12 health class. Some specific examples of these developments included:

- co-developing a four-square grid to help the students break down readings so they could use headings to guide their summaries
- co-construction of a writing frame and planning chart to make the requirements of the students' formative and summative writing more apparent to them and to help students organise their ideas more logically and coherently
- re-development of an internal assessment activity to make the language easier to access, and the development of a practice exam.

Across the units taught throughout the year, the health teacher used these supports and grew in confidence to develop her own resources to support the students' literacy skills. Consequently, the students' overall learning and NCEA achievement improved. As part of her mentoring of students, she also provided lunchtime study sessions, often providing kai (food) for the students, creating a welcoming environment.

As a result of her positive mentoring, her priority learners had high attendance in health classes, were engaged in the units of work and achieved well in NCEA, including externally (Achieved or better grades, including one Merit course endorsement). The pedagogical changes were designed to help her priority learners. But there were also gains for other students in the class. For example, after the changes, all of the students in this class indicated that they would continue with health as a subject in Year 13 and that the support and guidance provided by the teacher were appreciated very much. Consequently the teacher's confidence in trying out new approaches in the classroom increased.

This was a clear example of how teachers tend to grow professionally when they experience success with TAI. By working closely with the subject facilitator, this health teacher also improved her understanding of the requirements of the Level 2 NCEA health achievement standards and gained a deeper knowledge and development of skills related to literacy as it related, and could be applied, to learning senior health. She appreciated the importance of digging deeper to find out more about students' strengths and needs in order to respond accordingly.

Focusing on pedagogical changes

One of the key enablers of student achievement was when teachers made deliberate efforts to find out more about their students' needs by either talking in a more in-depth way with students or by looking more closely at the work produced by their priority learners. When teachers were clearer with students about what they were trying to achieve as teachers, students responded favourably. Often it motivated students because they saw that the teacher valued her/his teaching (and their learning) enough to make changes.

For example, a science teacher commented about how, when she indicated more specifically to students why she was asking them to work in groups, it seemed to make a difference, especially in supporting the students who seemed less interested in science.

Success story: Science teacher

I gave the students in my alternative Year 11 science class a formative [task] for the Physics Investigation. They all got Not Achieved [NCEA grade] but some of them were very close to Excellence ... they just had missed a few of the Achieved criteria. As a result I made up a survey to find out which parts of the investigation they needed more teaching around and summarised this data for the class. I then postponed the summative assessment and retaught the aspects of the standard which the students had identified as needing help with. Nearly all the students [got an] Achieved [grade] plus there were 4 Excellence grades and 2 Merits in a class of 12 students. I have put the students into mixed ability groups, which is probably nothing new but I think I have been more explicit [with the students] about the different strategies I have trialled. … This makes the students feel I really care about their learning. Because of this, two of the focus students, who began the year saying, 'I can't do science', are now very interested and surprising themselves with their level of achievement. One of these students now sits next to a high-achieving student, which helps.

It is unlikely that these students would have sat together without the intervention of the teacher to mix the students up, and more frequently than she had done previously. When interviewed, her students also indicated that she cared about their progress and that she was trying new ways of teaching and learning to help them specifically.

Another science teacher decided to find out why students did not achieve in a practical experiment in his Year 11 class. Since this was the first formally assessed practical investigation the class had done for the year, the teacher decided it was really important to guide the students more carefully through each stage of planning, carrying out the experiment, analysing and report-writing. This was an instance of where a teacher sought more specific data or information about why his students were not achieving and shared this information with the students. Some students commented that this was a change. Previously the teacher had tried to work out what his students needed, but he had not shared this with his students and certainly not in terms of the details of what they were good at and what they needed help with. The students commented that it was like they could improve the outcome together since they knew what they needed to do.

Some teachers identified particular ways they changed their relationships with students through showing they cared about what interested the students and how they could improve their learning. Often classes used differentiated task sheets depending on students' interests or ability levels. Feedback from students to teachers was also more enabled through the use of Google Docs, sometimes on a daily basis.

> "Students also mentioned in several schools that the criteria for assessments had become clearer recently. This, they said, was a key enabler to them achieving higher grades."

Students who were interviewed also appreciated the ability to comment on what was working for them in their learning progressions. The value of student voice was beginning to be realised in all three case study schools. This was evident in the fact that the students thought teachers were providing a lot more detailed feedback than they had received at primary school, and they had better relationships with their teachers at high school because they felt at ease about asking their teachers for help. The students agreed that their teachers were generally pushing them to do their best.

Students also mentioned in several schools that the criteria for assessments had become clearer recently. This, they said, was a key enabler to them achieving higher grades. Previously they may have not understood what the NCEA questions were asking, nor what was required exactly to get to Merit or Excellence levels for NCEA assessments. As a result, planned discussions about the wording of the questions and why sample answers met particular criteria really helped students to grasp what was required.

Narratives as support for inquiry

> "There were light-bulb moments about how small changes can make a difference."

As part of this project teachers were asked by their facilitators to write success stories. Reflecting on and sharing success stories, as well as how they made modifications to similar interventions in subsequent years, has helped other teachers to consider how they might approach or apply TAI. Sharing specific stories about specific learners also enabled other teachers of these learners to 'see' these students from another teacher's perspective. Sharing information about how individual students were learning in subjects gave teachers insights into how these focus students could be supported to achieve better. In other words, there was some transfer of information about the progress of individual students. Teachers in one of the case study schools indicated that this helped them to get to know their students better. It also challenged their views about these students as learners, and what they might be capable of.

When teachers shared how they undertook TAI with others, they not only became more aware of specific teaching and learning approaches to address a specific issue, but they also became more aware of the change cycles—the multiple possibilities for focus and implementation of TAI. There were light-bulb moments about how small changes can make a difference. Cycles of slight alterations to teaching can refine and enable more effective implementation of the changes to achieve or progress the learning goals (Conner, 2013; Kaser & Halbert, 2014. In Chapter 6 we discuss how when staff shared their learning there was a stronger likelihood of overall improved quality of educational outcomes across the school.

> *"Several staff talked about the buzz they got when they tried something new and it worked. Experiencing success and sharing this with other staff was important."*

Taking this one step further, Fullan and Hargreaves (2012) strongly advocate that in order to develop a high-quality education system, there needs to be a system-wide process for developing professional capital. TAI, when shared, can contribute to this process. The powerful professional learning that can result from shared TAI comes from teachers looking at multiple examples and contributing further ideas. Through teachers sharing their responses to students' issues in light of their implementation and success (Hargreaves, 1994; Muijs et al., 2004), and in response to the students' observable outcomes (Timperley, 2011a, 2011b), capability is increased and overall capacity for professional learning is enhanced.

Several staff talked about the buzz they got when they tried something new and it worked. Experiencing success and sharing this with other staff was important. Also, through sharing their stories about TAI implementation, teachers became aware that not everything always goes according to plan. The culture within the schools had to develop to the point where teachers valued each other's contributions and trusted each other not to belittle their stories or development as a teacher. A culture of trust (and humility) has been shown to be extremely important for sharing to be valued and leveraged for learning among groups (Covey, 2006). This should not be underestimated, and it was potentially a shift in the collaborative learning culture in these schools. The teachers had to feel comfortable with this approach. In one school, several teachers left the school because they felt uncomfortable doing TAI and sharing their practice.

Many previous studies have discussed establishing communities of professional practice among teachers. It is not the intention of this book to summarise this literature. However, in Chapter 5 we provide further insights into how cultures of professional learning were set up and maintained in the case study schools in this project.

Feedback loops for evaluating TAI

Success implementing TAI depends on teachers using information about students' learning to inform their practice and ongoing modifications to their teaching (Figure 1, see p. 2). In this project, teachers needed to be actively encouraged to be learners of their own practice, as Levin (2003) has advocated for continuous professional learning. Ideally, facilitated reflection on practice and student achievement outcomes can help teachers to identify *what* teaching behaviours make a difference, *how* they can be further enhanced, and *when* they make a difference. However, some of the vignettes indicate that what worked with some students one year may not have the same advantages for different students in subsequent years.

Teachers' knowledge of their students and their learning needs was crucial to the success of pedagogical change for improving students' success. They had to consider multiple ways to find out this information—through student work examples, talking to students, observing the learning behaviours of their priority learners, and using assessment information. As Kaser and Halbert (2014, p. 215) state, "Inquiry actions can only be considered good if significant learner outcomes have improved". We acknowledge that subjective outcomes such as enthusiasm are hard to measure. Teachers came up with a wide range of ways they could find out what their students were good at and what they needed help with, but there is huge scope to improve how this knowledge is used to inform both individual teachers' responses to learner needs, and how it is shared to build wider capability.

The facilitators discussed ideas and suggested ways teachers could collect evidence to evaluate how changes in teaching might influence their students' outcomes. Because teachers chose their own focus for inquiry in relation to their priority learners' needs, there was a wide range of ways they evaluated their teaching and learning successes. Therefore, consistency in evidence sources was not apparent (even within subject departments) and is one of the compromises involved in allowing teachers to initiate changes based on their students' needs. In future the teachers may discuss, and agree ahead of time, the sources that will be used to determine the degrees of change.

Feedback on teaching can occur through individual reflection, group dialogues, follow-up group processes, students' comments, and when facilitators support feedback and feed-forward. Feedback loops will only be useful if sufficient time and effort have been devoted to considering next steps based on the evidence. Muijs et al. (2004) have indicated that it takes significant on-the-job practice and support for new practice to become habitual.

We found that teachers in their second year of inquiry had a much more focused approach and understanding of what they could do as TAI. Once they realised it was not an extra or something new, and that as professionals they had an obligation to improve the outcomes of their students, they were more willing to take risks than previously, and seemed more willing to persist in implementing ongoing spirals of change.

Working in teams is not always easy, because there may be competing agendas and different levels of knowledge and expertise among the team. There was some frustration among staff in the case study schools where team or departmental processes seemed to be at odds with focusing on priority learners.

Summary

TAI as a process helped teachers in this project to develop a deeper understanding and enactment of "knowing the students' strengths and learning needs". When teachers deliberately and continuously rechecked this knowledge to inform the iterations of TAI, students saw that teachers cared about their progress and they responded to the information the teachers shared with them. Demonstrating the value of caring was very important. Keeping perspective, in terms of making changes that would improve the outcomes for targeted students, seemed to increase the chances that teachers' changes would have the desired effect. There were many things that teachers identified they could do. Focusing on what might make the most difference was important in keeping perspective.

It seemed that because teachers looked deeper at the needs of a small number of priority learners within NCEA classes, they were able to identify these students' needs and respond accordingly—both more immediately and more specifically. As Timperley, Kaser and Halbert (2014, p. 10) note, "Focused and deep rather than scattered and shallow is the goal". The teachers developed carefully constructed goals and implementation plans and actions, as well as evaluation of what went well and what didn't go so well. As a result, in the case study schools there were improvements for engagement data (e.g. in terms of attending class or participation in NCEA assessments) and in achievement data, probably due to a culture of continuous cycles of changes to teaching over a relatively short period of time.

Sharing success required a culture of trust that took time to establish. The facilitators, school leaders and teachers all played a role in establishing a culture in which curiosity about teaching and learning was stimulated, advanced and sustained. There are cultural considerations that leaders need to take into account to create professional trust among staff. These are discussed further in Chapters 5 and 6.

Guiding questions

1. What light-bulb moments have you had in your teaching?
2. Do you or other teachers share how you make decisions about teaching and learning experiences with your students? What difference might this make?
3. How do teachers in your school or centre currently manage TAI? How could you refine this to make TAI more manageable?
4. How can a culture of professional learning be enhanced in your centre or school?

Chapter 3: Case studies

Characteristics of the case study schools

The Secondary Student Achievement project required schools to focus on priority learners. As a result, all of the case study schools had a distinct focus on success for Māori. This included school-wide support for incorporating tikanga as part of everyday teaching, a strong kapa haka presence, a senior Māori student leadership programme, increasing the number of students who are speakers of te reo Māori or who are learning it, and increasing participation by whānau. Connecting with people (tangata) and communities was a strong element of each of these three schools' philosophies. This played out in the development of policy, decisions about how to implement TAI and the sharing of success stories. The case study schools were well on the way to embedding TAI because of their strong commitment to improving outcomes for their learners, and the fact that they had experienced success with TAI as a way to make this happen.

The leaders of these schools were very committed to making a difference for their priority groups. Not only did they all have strong visions for the outcomes they wanted for their learners, but they also had revised school policies and practices to enable the implementation of systemic strategic changes to enhance students' achievement. The point here is that they all had multiple strategies and targets, but they managed them by prioritising and identifying subtasks so that they could be implemented in a timely manner. They were also prepared to alter and adjust processes and events to refine implementation.

These leaders were very aware that their own school context mattered. While they knew their school could learn from the experiences of what worked for another school, they realised that the processes were not necessarily directly transferrable and that processes may need some adaptation for their school. Some examples of this are provided in the three school case studies that follow.

The three schools studied for these in-depth examples of practices had all been involved in the project for more than a year. They were selected because the lead facilitators had identified these schools as making good progress with TAI across a range of learning areas so it was becoming embedded practice and they were willing to participate. We wanted to be able to describe examples of where TAI was working well.

The overarching research question for the case studies was:

> How are teachers enabled to use teaching as inquiry (TAI) to meet the needs of their priority students and improve achievement?

In the wider project, NCEA achievement data was collected as an indicator of achievement shifts within schools. While we know there is not a direct cause and effect link between PLD and student outcomes, we present this data for each school in this chapter to show how the shifts in achievement occurred.

In addition, two senior leaders from two of the case study schools were invited to summarise their school's progress at a facilitator hui (meeting) for the whole facilitation team (of 20) in July 2014. Notes were taken at these presentations, and these informed the background and questions for the interviews at the schools.

Also, in each case study school we conducted focus group interviews with the senior leaders, teachers and students. Audio recordings of these interviews were transcribed and thematically analysed to derive the themes that are discussed in Chapter 6. The cases were developed from the focus group interviews, observations, facilitator reports, ERO reports and success stories of practice-based interventions, alongside student achievement data. They are discussed in terms of progress and success factors at multiple levels: whole school, department or faculty, and individual teacher.

The facilitators' written reports, which contributed to each milestone report to the Ministry, were also used to substantiate the schools' claims about progress and to provide specific examples of teacher professional learning and consequent student learning to support our findings.

The subject-specific facilitators asked teachers to provide either written or oral vignettes or success stories. In phase two of this study, during 2015, the facilitators were also asked to contribute success stories. These have contributed to our narrative inquiry approach (Clandinin & Connelly, 2000), whereby the experiences, as written, were used to probe deeper into the words and practices of the teachers, leaders and facilitators in order to contribute to a better understanding of the how and why of what transpired.

Mostly these stories were corroborated by another story (e.g. teachers' accounts with students' interviews, or leaders' accounts with facilitators' accounts) so that the credibility of the claims was able to be checked. Such questions as 'Is a particular interpretation to be believed?' or 'Is this example consistent with practice?' or 'Is this supported in the literature?' helped us to scrutinise the information. These examples of teachers', facilitators' and leaders' contributions appear as inserts throughout the book. This is so that the voices of the participants can provide insights into their practice changes for others to share and consider in relation to their own practice.

All of the data sources described above were compared with more extensive cases of teachers' development as they engaged in successive cycles of TAI. These comparisons enabled us to investigate the enablers and potential barriers of the implementation of the project at its multiple levels, including school learning communities, departments/faculties, individuals and groups of teachers, and priority learners. Iterations of the school cases and aspects of this book were collaboratively generated by the facilitation team, and members checked with the senior leaders of the case study schools.

Sorting out what makes a difference

As previously indicated, the New Zealand education context itself provides a driver for both TAI and focusing on the needs of priority students. We considered previous indicators of structures and processes that might enable professional learning. An ERO report (ERO, 2014) had identified five main enablers of professional learning in schools in

New Zealand, and these enablers seemed reasonable to use as a framework to categorise the cases. The enablers identified were:

- external drivers
- structural and procedural enablers
- developmental enablers
- achievement enablers
- contextual enablers.

External drivers included external forces that schools need to respond to, such as compliance with the New Zealand Qualifications Authority (NZQA), the 2012 teacher accreditation requirements of the New Zealand Teachers Council, marketisation influences on education, and international trends. In New Zealand secondary schools the pressures of multiple curriculum outcomes and the perceived demand for students to achieve NCEA results often lead teachers to focus on coverage of content rather than depth of understanding that connects with students interests.

Structural and procedural enablers were those that facilitated or engaged staff and communities within the institution to become aware of, and work towards, embedding learning outcomes. They appeared to have inter-related functions. Structural enablers were the tangible institutional arrangements such as committees, key management positions, plans and policies that were set up to support educational processes and facilitate institutional change. Procedural enablers were the mandated activities that facilitated the implementation of plans and policies and provided feedback data. The effectiveness of the structural enablers lay in the way they were related systemically to processes that enabled the implementation of the espoused policy and practices. This meant the appointments and committees became procedural enablers when roles included authority to implement and monitor formal and informal curriculum and quality-assurance functions.

Developmental enablers were those that assisted staff or programme teams to undertake curriculum development. They included a clear articulation of the school's goals and philosophies about teaching and learning, the engagement of staff in professional learning, the identification of 'champions', implementing specific projects and recognition of the time required for change.

Achievement enablers related to how students were assisted to achieve. Flexible delivery methods and curriculum frameworks that focus on students were found to be the most effective.

Contextual enablers related to the willingness of staff and students to conduct the other enablers (e.g. the emotional health of the school, including staff morale and confidence in themselves and their leadership). Examples included creating space for staff to think, the type of communication strategies used, whether there was a clear institutional culture with a focus on teaching and learning, and the provision of positive feedback.

The following sections provide the three school case studies. First, each school's context, leadership characteristics and focus for inquiry are described. This is followed by a discussion of the external drivers, structural and procedural enablers, developmental enablers, achievement enablers and contextual enablers as a framework for discussing the factors that influenced the implementation of TAI in these schools.

School A

Description of the school

This co-educational secondary school is situated in a fast-growing population area in Canterbury that describes itself as being "small enough to care and large enough to compete". It highly values its role as an inclusive school that receives and gives support to its community. Leaders of the school are actively involved in promoting the profile of the school, particularly within a cluster of local schools involved in improving educational achievement in the area.

The school strives to motivate and inspire all students to achieve their best and to become adults who contribute to their community. The core values are "respect, integrity, community and excellence".

A recent ERO report indicated that the school had progressed well in developing teaching practices, use of achievement information, student leadership and success as Māori. Staff are increasingly using achievement information to foster positive changes to learners' engagement, progress and achievement. There is a positive trend in improvement for all national achievement assessment data, including the number of students obtaining Scholarships. There is also additional targeted support for students with special needs, which seems to be supporting them as well as building a culture that success is possible for all students.

The school is seen to play an important role in contributing to the leadership and promotion of Māori culture in the local area. Leaders, staff and students are all contributing to success for Māori as Māori through a strong kapa haka presence, a senior Māori student leadership programme, an increasing number of students who are speakers of te reo Māori, or who are learning it, increased participation by whānau, and tuakana–teina relationships where older students support and mentor younger students.

Leadership

The principal of this school is very committed to building leadership capacity within the school. He is very supportive of TAI, to the extent that he undertook his own inquiry in 2013 and found it to be a very useful process. He has taken a firm stand that all staff should be involved in TAI and does not sign off on teacher registration renewal unless the staff person has engaged in inquiry. The outcomes and learning from inquiry are used as part of the appraisal system within the school. There is also clear tracking and reporting of student outcomes to the board of trustees, which is supported by a database manager. Departments are using this information to scrutinise how much they are teaching and how they might adjust their practices to be more effective.

The principal considered that TAI worked really well in 2013 for some staff because there was a clear focus on pedagogy. There has been some sharing at a departmental level about successes as a result of the teachers' inquiries. The school is working towards sharing inquiry processes and outcomes more widely and held a full staff meeting facilitated by the teachers in 2013. Departmental sharing occurred in the Science and Social Science learning areas in 2014. Other learning areas, such as Health, PE and Mathematics, are developing their shared understanding of TAI.

Focus for inquiry

The facilitators used the following questions to support their work with the teachers in all subject specialties within the school to address the dimensions of concern:

The knowledge and skills I as a teacher have and need.
- *What do I already know that I can use to improve outcomes for my students?*
- *What do I need to learn to do to improve outcomes for my students?*
- *What sources of evidence/knowledge can I utilise to find out about my knowledge and practices?*
- *What evidence do I have of my own learning needs?*

Deepen professional knowledge and refine professional skills.
- *Where can I go to get support to develop my knowledge and skills?*
- *Who can I get support from in and out of school to help me?*
- *What professional readings would be useful?*
- *Do I know how my students learn?*

Engage students in new learning experiences.
- *How and why am I changing my approach, trying new strategies, differentiating?*
- *How am I using new digital technologies to engage my students in learning?*
- *How am I building on existing knowledge and skills to create new learning?*
- *How do I ensure that learning experiences meet the needs of all learners (diverse identities, languages and cultures)?*

The departments supported by subject specialists in the school are science, social science, health/PE and maths. As an example of a department that has embraced TAI, the whole science department is focusing on building students' literacy, but with their specific priority students' needs in mind. The teachers' use of multiple strategies in 2013 seemed to make a big difference to students' engagement and understanding in science. The backgrounds of the students who were the focus of the teachers in these departments at School A are given in Table 1.

Table 1: Backgrounds of students who were the subject of inquiry at School A

Number of Māori	Number of Pasifika	Number of ELLs	Number of SEN	Number of students below curriculum level/NCEA	Number of students at curriculum level/NCEA	Number of students above the curriculum level/NCEA
9	5	2	9	13	9	3

Note: ELLs are English Language Learners—these are students who have another language as their first language. SEN are special education needs students.

The data in Table 1 only reflect the number of students who were the focus of their teachers' inquiries. That is, teachers considered the learning needs of these priority learners specifically when redesigning their teaching.

As a result of identifying each student's strengths and weaknesses, the science teachers reconsidered the amount of content they cover for NCEA Level 1 and whether, as a department, they were trying to push too much into one year. This led to the reduction of the number of standards (assessments) in science offered at Year 11 (NCEA Level 1). For the junior science classes the department focus is on getting the students engaged with science. Teachers are using a variety of types of formative assessment and breaking examples of summative (NCEA) tasks into smaller, more targeted and more manageable activities.

For some of these tasks the students are given marking schedules separately for each smaller section of each assessment. Then either peers or the teachers provide feedback for each section of the assessments separately. This, the students said, enabled them "to digest the feedback in smaller bites", so there was more chance they would improve in each section of work. The teachers have noticed that this approach has been especially helpful for the science inquiry-based standards.

Some specific examples of teachers' changes to their teaching shed light on how small changes can improve student outcomes. One of the science teachers, who had the top class, was focusing on how her English-as-second-language students who were "in trouble with vocab" could be assisted. She purposefully designed literacy tasks that have raised their level of achievement.

Another example is where a social science teacher identified that three of her students were writing answers to assessment items seemingly "without thinking about what was required or asked by the question". In response, she introduced some structured literacy activities with the support and guidance of the social studies facilitator. The teacher created literacy templates, sentence starters and activities for structured thinking so that students' answers would flow better. She has also let parents know about the topics they have been covering in social science and "flicked them an email" to notify parents when there was a test coming up. As a result, two of the students who were not achieving gained a Merit in a test. The social science teacher commented that:

> [Paying] attention for these kids is difficult but learning has increased. The parent contact seems to be useful and I've had good feedback at the parent interviews about the emails [prior to tests]. (Social science teacher)

Another social science teacher identified that her priority students were not able to understand the questions in the school- level common tests. With help from her facilitator, she devised ways to enable her students to write more concise paragraphs, to use appropriate punctuation, and to communicate better by constructing more effective sequences and a better flow of key ideas. She also provided more opportunities and practice with specific literacy techniques, which seemed to be help students to increase their awareness and understanding of what to include when writing paragraphs. She noted that her students are able to speak English orally but need support to translate this to text using conventional good writing structures. Surprisingly, students did not take up her offer to complete the assessments orally as an alternative to the written assessment, even though they were well aware that they might get different marks if they were given the opportunity to be assessed differently.

As a result of students not seeming to be very motivated, a PE teacher developed a tracking/goal sheet for assessment units in his Year 13 class. He supported students to develop their literacy skills as well as breaking down assessment tasks into smaller subtasks and using checklists for students more often. He has also been using digital activities and resources to help students develop critical thinking and literacy skills by being more explicit and adapting assessment tasks to suit learners' interests.

Two teachers of Year 11 mathematics have been focusing their inquiries on literacy in statistics. One of these maths teachers has focused on improving visual representations and encouraging his students to communicate more in-depth thinking, along with improving their literacy skills. An excerpt from the maths facilitator report summary for this school stated:

> Both teachers have gained a deeper understanding of how this standard might be assessed. They are more aware of the specific language required for this [achievement] standard and are using appropriate technology to support the learning of their students. As a result the success rate for this standard is likely to be much higher than in past years. … [Another maths teacher] has focused her inquiry around the essential skill of 'managing self'. She is explicitly emphasising this in all her work with her Year 10 class. At the same time she is recognising the individual needs of the students in the class and is planning and developing resources that are interesting, relevant and that will engage the students.

As an example of how a maths teacher was trying to make activities more engaging, students commented that she was always trying to make their learning in maths relevant to them and often used fun activities such as the 'fly swat' paired activity on the board to physically identify answers. They appreciated that she cared enough to create interesting ways for them to learn.

Building a community of learners

As part of TAI implementation in this school, we observed that the teachers did not usually read the research literature on learning and teaching without prompting. During the initial phases of TAI the teachers and school leaders relied on the facilitators to indicate some pertinent readings or to help them interpret the literature. As in the other two case study schools, the teachers agreed that they do not know what is out there (to read) and needed the guidance and support—or the help—of the discriminatory eye of the facilitators to recommend good examples of research and inquiry activities for TAI that they could use to "spark their thinking".

TAI requires developing a deeper understanding and enactment of "knowing the students' strengths and learning needs" and continually rechecking this knowledge during iterations, including identifying what aspects teachers needed or what tools to use as they dared to step into their inquiry. Many of the teachers chose to focus on classes in the senior school because they knew the importance of helping students to achieve better grades. This in itself was an external driver, as discussed in the next section.

External drivers

All of the teachers in the focus group were well aware of the external drivers for students to achieve in NCEA assessments. Senior leaders in School A commented on how they and middle leaders had improved their knowledge and understanding of how TAI could be used to improve students' achievement. NCEA results were often used by teachers as indicators of success. For example, several teachers indicated that because they helped students to "unpick" the language used in the questions for NCEA, there was an increase in pass rates.

They have seen its impact specifically in the school NCEA Level 1 achievement data during 2012 and 2013 (Table 2). By focusing on a small number of priority learners within NCEA classes, there were shifts in success over a relatively short period of time for both engagement data (e.g. attending class) and achievement in NCEA assessments. This can be seen in the data in Table 2, which shows the achievement data for students in NCEA Levels 1 and 2 in 2012 and 2013.

Table 2: Level 1 and Level 2 NCEA achievement data for students at School A, 2012 and 2013

		Percentage with NCEA Level 1 or above		Percentage with NCEA Level 2 or above	
		2012	2013	2012	2013
Māori	Total	84.2	95.2	63.2	61.9
Pasifika	Total	x	x	x	x
NZ European/Pākehā	Total	72.2	89.8	62.6	78

There was a slight increase in the percentage of Māori achievement for NCEA Level 1 between 2012 and 2013. This also corresponded to a higher achievement overall for NCEA achievement for NZ European/Pākehā students at this school over the same time period.

Figure 2 represents Time 1 and Time 2 data for the students at School A. Time 1 data is the predicted achievement and Time 2 is the actual achievement of students. This shows a clearer trend in terms of the shifts in levels of achievement of students, and that Māori and Pasifika students tended to show gains in achievement at T2 than what had been predicted at T1. There was also a shift in expected gains in achievement for all students.

Figure 2: School A: students' predicted achievement (T1) and actual achievement (T2) in NCEA Level 1, 2014. The y-axis is number of students. The x-axis is the level of achievement according to NCEA criteria, N – not achieved, A – Achieved, M – Merit, E – Excellence.

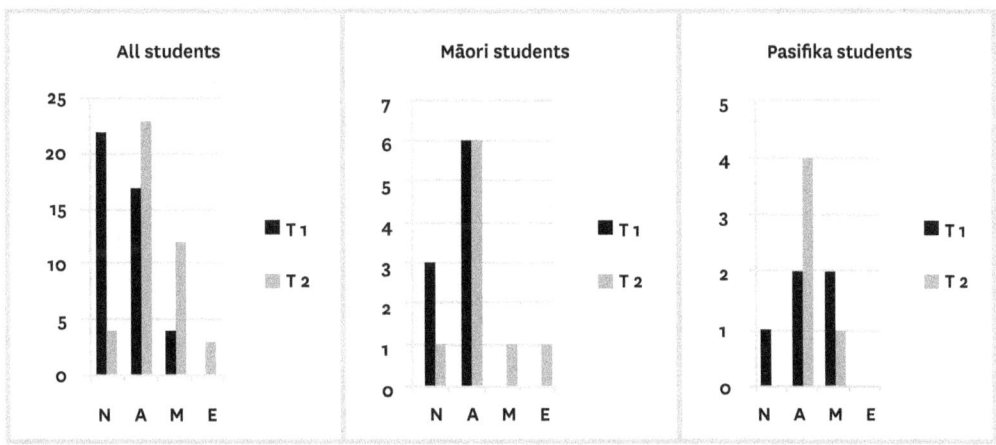

The achievement shifts in Figure 2 indicate that there was an improvement in NCEA outcomes for Māori and Pasifika students, both in the decrease in the number of students who did not achieve (N) and the increase in those who moved from Achieved grades (A) to Merit (M) and Excellence levels (E). These changes are not all attributed to the engagement of the school with TAI. However, we discuss the various aspects of the enablers for this school in the next sections and how the leaders and staff were convinced that TAI processes were certainly part of the reason students were achieving better at this school.

Structural and procedural enablers

Most of the structural and procedural enablers were related to prioritising TAI and allocating time to make sure teachers were able to focus on their own inquiry processes. For example, some staff from this school took a professional learning day each term to spend time with their respective subject specialist facilitators on campus at the University of Canterbury. This worked well because the teachers had a specific focus for the day, such as preparing new resources, or they spent time turning NCEA exemplars into smaller and more manageable teaching and learning activities.

While some teachers have developed new resources, many have claimed that they do not get sufficient time to prepare literacy tasks during their usual teaching preparation time at the school. Effective preparation for NCEA internal assessment development takes a lot of time, especially since teachers have been designing new tasks for the realignment of the NCEA standards with the curriculum.

To support this ongoing development, some of the facilitators provided teachers with templates for constructing literacy-rich activities for their subject areas. Once teachers were provided with the initial ideas and associated pedagogical understanding about setting up and using the activities, they saw how an activity worked. When they had a basic template, they were more willing to adapt it to new situations and create related tasks for themselves. They needed the initial impetus, and then some support for implementation with their classes. As one facilitator said:

> The [literacy] activity is something that they really need our help with. One of the key things that both science teachers said was that once we have given them the resources for a particular activity/strategy, and they have tried it and seen positive responses from students, then they can adapt the activity to other contexts—using the same ideas/approaches.

A key procedural enabler was when teachers made deliberate efforts to find out more about their students by either talking more in depth with students or connecting with families and whānau. In this school, weekly learning reports for Years 9 and 10 students are sent home. This was considered to be a useful strategy for communicating with parents and for tracking students' progress. The account of how this led to improved outcomes is given by a teacher who was in the second year of TAI.

Success story: Teacher in second year of TAI

One of my focus students really wasn't engaged at the beginning of the year. I tried to get as much background information about him as I could. I talked with his dean, I talked with his parents, and I talked with him. I then had a meeting with him and his dean and we looked at how we might be able to make science more enjoyable and relevant for him. He changed his attitude in class and began to become involved in class activities. I think [this was] because I took the time to find out about him—what was going on for him—and ... I was genuinely interested in helping him to do better. Maybe that was it—maybe he saw me take an interest and has met me partway. It's still not all easy, but he's making an effort and has definitely improved.

Developmental enablers

The first year of TAI in this school was trialled with five teachers who were willing to 'give it a go'. The principal commented at the focus group with the teachers and facilitators:

> It would be really easy to give it away in the first year. I don't think you guys [facilitators] put that up front enough—that we wouldn't see a difference in the first year.

However, he did agree that the shifts in teachers' thinking about the depth of focus and thinking required were considerable for some teachers.

Some teachers who were in their second year of using TAI realised that they needed to focus more than previously on what supports students to learn, and that they needed to help students make connections between disparate ideas. They found that their assumptions about what students found useful, how students learn and what they need became more apparent as they focused on specific strategies for helping students to understand concepts. In other words, they were looking more specifically at the outcomes of their learners, or what they produced, to figure out what their students' needs were. For example, the vignette of a science teacher below describes how her thinking about what helped the students changed as a result of seeking their responses and feedback about what worked for them.

Reflection: Science teacher

I have been focusing on developing my students' understanding of the Nature of Science and to develop their science capabilities. They had been learning about the circulatory system and the heart. I wanted them to think about the different representations that we had used to help them to understand the structure and function of the heart (dissection, diagrams, pulse rate activity, jigsaw, animations). I also wanted them to think about what the representations could be missing and how they could be improved. The activity I gave them worked really well and the students were very engaged and thought carefully about the representation and also about their own learning. Even students who did not usually like writing much put a lot of thought and effort into it. I realised that one of the activities that I thought would help them the most was their least favorite. It seems that they struggled to make links between that activity and how the heart worked so I need to have more discussion around this with my students next year. I will also think about using this strategy with other concepts such as models of electricity. It highlighted that what I think will help them with their learning is not always the case so it's really important to get feedback and evaluations on specific sections of their work to get an idea of what helps their learning and identify gaps.

Some teachers visited other schools to observe good practices and discussed overall year and unit plans (for science) with other subject specialists. There was also ongoing encouragement for teachers to visit each other during teaching episodes, but this has not happened very frequently in this school and could be enhanced in future years.

Achievement enablers

The subject specialist facilitators mostly used questions to help drive teacher review and actions, as indicated above. These questions provided a focus for zooming in on what the teachers had identified was important for the students and helped them to be self-reflective. The teachers interviewed indicated that they were able to focus on achievement data and other observable outcomes from formative assessment tasks to help them consider changes to their practice, and then monitor what effect these changes had on students' understanding.

Students who were part of the focus group indicated a number of ways teachers showed they cared about their progress and achievement. For example, they mentioned that teachers provided a lot more detailed feedback than they got at primary school, and that they had better relationships with their teachers because they felt at ease going to their teachers for help. All of the students in the focus group said that often there were differentiated task sheets, depending on students' ability levels. Students noted that the criteria for assessments had become clearer. They were also pleased that if they had been sick during an assessment, reassessment opportunities were offered.

Contextual enablers

This school was fortunate to be relatively close to the university so that the facilitators could either visit the school easily or the teachers could take time out to come to the university to work on new resource development and have discussions with their subject specialists. This was not the case for the other two schools profiled (Schools B and C).

Teachers commented that some of the resources developed and shared by the subject specialist facilitators were amazing. In particular, support with developing new subject-specific literacy task sheets or online activities helped the teachers to work out what students did not understand regarding the structure and language used for specific assessment tasks. The teachers could see that the information they were gaining about students' learning, or their gaps in learning, were supplemented by students completing these targeted tasks. This information helped to build teachers' confidence so that they could identify specific students' needs and design tasks to help students develop their skills appropriately.

Teachers claimed that they also gained satisfaction with TAI when they recognised that small changes in their approaches to teaching led to improved student outcomes. This was because they had identified the specific learning needs of their priority learners (which may be very different for different individuals within a group) and had been assisted to make changes to address these needs.

The principal commented that he had seen a huge difference between teachers who had only just begun in the inquiry cycle and those who were part of the original group and therefore had more experience. This indicates that not only is time needed to develop teachers' skills in using TAI, but there is a developmental aspect that needs to be taken into account for implementing TAI. This probably relates to experience with success, and the consequent teacher efficacy that is connected with having success (Bandura, 1997). This is discussed further under the heading "Incremental versus large-scale change" in Chapter 5.

Barriers to implementation of TAI in School A

Teachers at this school indicated that time for them to reflect and time to document the changes they made to their teaching was very precious. This related to the amount of time they spent planning their teaching versus time to do their administrative tasks and meet other school-wide goals and agendas. So prioritising time to conduct TAI was seen as essential to its implementation and success. A science teacher commented on this:

> I don't have time to mould them [resources] for the type of class I have got.

As a consequence of recognising the importance of time for reflection, and identifying what resources would support literacy development, the science department is considering how they allocate time in order to prioritise the development of new teaching resources that specifically target the development of literacy in science contexts. As a result, they decided they needed to prioritise what they discussed and how long they discussed other ideas and issues at departmental meetings. They were finding other ways to disseminate information that seemed to take up precious meeting time.

Teachers who have been using TAI for several years in this school indicated that they have a clearer understanding of the processes involved. It took time for them to understand what they could do: they needed to try TAI a few times, with the support of the facilitators, so that they persisted if the results were not quite as they expected. For example, a science teacher commented that after his huge success in 2013 with his focus on literacy, and consequent improved overall student achievement (not just with his priority learners), he was surprised at how different his priority learner group was in 2014. In contrast, a relatively new teacher to the school indicated that he thought the students were lazy and not motivated and found this frustrating. He had not yet taken on board that his role was to find ways to make lessons relevant and interesting. This indicates there is a challenge for schools and facilitators in such projects to recognise how teachers' beliefs about their role and their relative success influence their actions.

The teachers in this school agreed that they initially needed support to progress their understanding of how students learn and what motivates students to engage with tasks. They also appreciated having someone to talk things through with when things did not go to plan or students' achievement did not appear to improve at first, so that they continued to be curious about how they could improve students' outcomes through their actions. Teachers' understanding about learning—where they considered what questions to ask about how to support specific priority learners— seemed to help them to be more targeted in their teaching. This implies that teachers needed to discover what individual students' needs are first in order to design strategies and interventions, or specific tasks to address these learning needs.

School B

This school became involved in the Secondary Student Achievement project in February 2013 through the participation of a couple of staff who wanted to raise the success of their priority students. Other teachers became involved in Term 3 of that year. Since then there have been five facilitators working in the school with 10 teachers. According to the liaison facilitator for the project, the teachers have become increasingly receptive to TAI, particularly as iterations of inquiry provided teachers with a sense of success, and as they realised that changes could lead to student achievement gains.

The liaison facilitator has used a *fading guidance* approach, where she has modelled a process of reflective coaching one to one with teachers. The specialist classroom teacher was present during these reflective coaching sessions and has gained confidence to support staff with TAI by asking prompting questions to guide their reflection.

Description of the school

This public girls' urban high school is in a small city (population approximately 30,000). The school has 420 students, comprising 17 percent Māori, 3 percent Pasifika, 5 percent Asian and 75 percent Pākehā/European. There are 35 staff members. The school has strong links with its community and with other schools in the city—especially the local boys' high school—for co-teaching some subjects such as statistics, te reo Māori and commerce subjects. The school also has an agreement with a local Catholic integrated school to share the teaching of French. There is a teenage parent unit on the school site that has been in existence for 2 years, as well as an early childhood education centre.

School philosophy

The school's mission statement says that it develops life-long learners through an inclusive and comprehensive education to prepare students to contribute to their communities, and for them to experience success. The school prides itself on providing an innovative education that encourages personal excellence and develops confident, caring, well-educated young women within a safe and supportive community. The school notes in its prospectus that it

> proudly maintains strong cultural traditions with an emphasis on self-motivation, high personal values, mutual respect and discipline …. Programmes are available to cater for the individual needs of girls at each level and to further expand their personal development in preparation for tertiary education or the workforce.

School culture

The culture of the school is based on its long customary history (over 134 years) and sound traditions. There is an effusive culture of students seemingly getting on with their work, but staff cannot always tell whether students are learning. The staff agreed that there were generally collegial and positive relationships among them. Some teachers offer additional tutoring outside of class time (e.g. in the lunch hour), especially for senior classes prior to NCEA exams. Students commented that staff care about their learning and take an interest in their activities outside of school. For example, there is a school-wide academic counselling initiative that has brought parents/whānau into the school alongside the learner to discuss academic progress and next steps. This initiative indicates to students that the teachers care about their progress.

The school is holding Kotahitanga days for Māori students each term, or for students who take te reo Māori or kapa haka. These days include an emphasis on te reo, tikanga and kapa haka, as well as providing information about career pathways and guest speakers. A climate of encouragement supports Māori students to develop personal goals, to seek support from friends and whānau, and to participate in extra tutoring if they want it. The school also employs a Māori support staff person, whom the students value and relate to well.

Teachers are also going out of their way to provide a climate of inclusiveness and belonging. For example, one of the Māori students indicated that it was very welcoming to be able to stay at lunchtime in the room where they learn te reo. Other students interviewed also appreciated the positive relationships they had with their teachers. For example, one student commented about her health teacher, "You can ask her *anything*", implying this went beyond their school work. Other students made comments such as "The teacher has a real passion", "Our teachers are still learning" and "Our teachers know what they are doing."

The school is endeavouring to make systemic changes that will support students' achievement, particularly in relation to making content relevant to students. As well, te reo Māori is being incorporated into class feedback, which is supported visually through posters on the classroom walls for phrases that teachers can use to give feedback to students. The teachers are trying to incorporate content into their courses that includes mātauranga Māori, but acknowledge they need support to do this more often and in a culturally appropriate way.

Leadership

The principal and senior team are committed to using the inquiry process for improving teaching and student achievement. The principal considers that it is really important to model the behaviour the leaders of the school want. There is no doubt that this is a team approach to enabling whole-school change. The two deputy principals support the link between TAI and the school's appraisal processes, and co-ordinate TAI across learning areas.

The senior leadership team acknowledged that some teachers were resistant early on. To help overcome this, on some occasions a member of the senior leadership team talked to these teachers individually about the TAI process to clarify any concerns. The leadership team also supported each other to stay positive. They acknowledged that it was natural to get some resistance in the early stages of a new initiative. During the second year of implementation, as understanding increased, the resistance levels dropped. The school leaders valued the need to clarify ideas about TAI with the staff, but also realised that they may not get a 100 percent of the staff feeling comfortable with using TAI.

Middle leaders in the school are taking on responsibility for improving student achievement. For example, two middle leaders, from the Health and Physical Education learning area, are focusing their inquiry on raising achievement for priority learners in two Year 13 classes. The teachers have used qualitative and quantitative information from their TAI cycles (each finding out about four priority learners' strengths and needs) to incorporate a range of strategies during their second year of implementation. They are continually adapting their approaches to meet the changing needs of their students as their priority learners develop skills at different rates.

In some departments, changes were made when planning for learning within units of work as well as in the pedagogy 'in the moment' of classroom interactions. For example, the middle leaders were:

- scaffolding learning activities and resources (through selection) to ensure greater access to and completion of tasks
- initiating the use of Google Docs to provide ongoing, effective feedback for formative learning tasks in the lead-up to summative (NCEA) assessments
- strategically selecting research/readings for learners to ensure they have quality sources as a starting point (when teachers created specific literacy activities, these enabled learners the opportunities to 'unpack' the readings in more depth; then teachers evaluated how well students achieved as a result of changing the way they taught)
- being responsive to learners' needs by offering some choice in learning tasks and creating new activities and contexts

- collecting student voice regularly to reflect on and refine learning experiences
- strengthening communication within the learning area by celebrating successes and discussing barriers, for which possible solutions were shared within the department.

Focus for inquiry

At School B there were very few Pasifika or English-as-second-language students who were the focus of teachers' inquiries. Table 3 provides a summary of the types of priority students at this school.

Table 3: The number of students in School B identified as priority learners for TAI

Number of Māori	Number of Pasifika	Number of ELLs	Number of SEN	Number of students below curriculum level/NCEA	Number of students at curriculum level/NCEA	Number of students above the curriculum level/NCEA
21	1	1	3	16	16	7

Note: ELLs are English Language Learners—these are students who have another language as their first language. SEN are special education needs students

The targeted learning areas where teachers were supported by subject specialist facilitators for the 2 years of implementation are given in Table 4.

Table 4: Target subjects for facilitation at school B and the number of teachers involved

2013 focus		2014 focus	
Subject	No. of subject teachers	Subject	No. of subject teachers
Science	2	Science	2
Mathematics	1	English	2
English	2	Health	1
Economics	1	Home economics	1
History	1	History	1
		Languages	3

According to the leaders and teachers interviewed at this school, TAI has enabled the senior leaders, middle leaders and teachers to focus more specifically on what they need to change in terms of curriculum renewal and pedagogical considerations. The middle leaders acknowledged that as a result of undertaking TAI they have been more reflective in (and on) their teaching and have worked hard to create a range of activities and learning experiences that are more customised to learners' needs, especially in relation to literacy and understanding what is required for assessments. Where possible, they used a range of evidence, including feedback from students (student voice), to identify what changes were needed and to evaluate the impact of their changes in practice.

> *"Teachers used students' responses and questions to make adjustments to worksheets and reinforcement activities in (or during) teaching, which had a more targeted and immediate effect for student learning."*

Student voice was considered valuable for identifying issues and ongoing evaluation. Students' ideas were being used more often at this school to inform the TAI processes. Potentially there is scope to increase the range of ways, and frequency, that student voice can inform teaching. The use of Web 2.0 tools helped teachers to get ongoing feedback from students so that they were more aware of learning issues and needs as they arose. Teachers used students' responses and questions to make adjustments to worksheets and reinforcement activities in (or during) teaching, which had a more targeted and immediate effect for student learning.

In some departments and PLGs, observations of teaching were also encouraged. Two years ago some teachers were very averse to other teachers coming in to observe their teaching. There has been a huge shift in mindset for some teachers in terms of their thinking about continuous improvement and the idea that teachers can always improve the achievement of students. For some it was good to be reminded that you don't just teach subjects, you teach kids. A focus on what the students need was a new way of framing their teaching rather than focusing on what content they had to cover.

One of the science teachers discussed his focus on the NCEA achievement standards tasks for his Year 11 non-advancing in science class. He took on the philosophy that "the one who talks the most, learns the most", so he is trying to get the students to talk and interact with each other more and talk more than he does. He is also focusing on developing the girls' literacy using key terms, structured reading tasks and informal tests. Previously girls in this class had low confidence in understanding text. He said, "If I break it (the exam question) down, they get it more easily".

At the beginning of the year one of the science teachers observed that his Year 11 students who were reluctant readers would not read a whole page of text. He decided to provide chunks of text, and has slowly increased the amount of text he expects them to read throughout the year. Recently he praised the class for successfully reading a whole page of text.

There was a sense from all 10 teachers involved in their third year of TAI that compared with 2 years ago there was definitely a greater understanding of TAI among staff, and that TAI was now more closely aligned with intended learning outcomes and the school goals. All heads of department are more aware of the need to align formative assessments with learning outcomes.

Building a community of learners

The teachers and leaders in the school indicated that the facilitators were crucial in building expertise, providing curriculum guidance, and giving support and help with how to focus the inquiry process on priority learners. The facilitators were also seen to be reinforcing messages from the schools' leadership team. TAI is building momentum in this school now that it is being implemented at a whole-school level. Monday staff meetings include PLG time. Teachers are given release time to visit another class or to visit another school. As a result, there are structural changes that support the inquiry process, and these help staff to value TAI. The deputy principals have indicated that more sharing of examples of TAI, both within PLGs and at whole-staff meetings, will be a future focus.

There is also a sense that students in general are gaining agency for determining what they want and for identifying their learning needs. In support of this, the principal commented that "Students are now telling us when they think we are not meeting their needs. We still have a long way to go."

Goal setting for students is also coming to the fore—more frequently and across multiple learning areas. As one example of this, science students are filling in worksheets that help them to identify what they are doing well and what they need to work on. Therefore, teachers who shift their focus to purposefully designing tools to help students reflect on their learning are also supporting the building of the community of learners in this school. This is because reflective learning is becoming part of the culture of learning.

External drivers

A key external driver for this school was that staff identified the need to improve student achievement right across the school year levels. Although the school had a focus on improving Year 9 achievement, the structures and pedagogical changes to enable this were not in place across the school in the second year of TAI implementation. According to one of the deputy principals, there were "pockets of promise" that had showed where teachers had made shifts in approaches to teaching.

In 2012 the senior leaders estimated that a third of the teachers knew what to do for TAI linked to developing better student outcomes. Since then they have utilised external comparisons of students' achievement with other local schools to emphasise the imperative for change. Initially not all staff agreed on the need for change. There was quite a bit of resistance, and many staff preferred to retain the status quo. However, NCEA results have been used to indicate the need to raise achievement, as indicated in Table 5. There were no Pasifika students undertaking NCEA levels 1 or 2 in 2011 and 2013 at this school. The data for 2013 were not separated by ethnicity.

Table 5: Percentage of students in School B achieving Level 1 and Level 2 NCEA, 2011 and 2013

		Percentage with NCEA Level 1 or above		Percentage with NCEA Level 2 or above	
		2011	2013	2011	2013
Māori	Total	62.5	x	50	x
NZ European/ Pākehā	Total	92.6	94.2	82.3	75.6

While the percentage of students achieving NCEA Level 1 and Level 2 is quite high, it is considerably lower for Māori students than for NZ European/Pākehā students. Therefore there is an equity issue in this school to redress this difference.

The school is competing with other schools in the same town for student enrolments. The senior leaders consider this indicates a need to provide high-quality educational experiences to sustain and improve the reputation of—and consequently the number of students at—this school. The school is monitoring its roll carefully but they know that their reputation (for achievement) will contribute to their ability to attract new students.

Structural and procedural enablers

School B developed several structural enablers alongside the drivers to support the implementation and development of TAI more widely. For example, initially PLGs were set up in 2013 and met regularly throughout the year. Common goals were also devised for all Year 9 classes. These were built into the teachers' appraisal system for 2013. The New Zealand Teachers Council's Teacher Registration Criteria were also used by the senior leaders as part of the focus for appraisal across the whole school, to emphasise the importance of how reflection and action within teaching can contribute to ongoing teachers' registration requirements.

The next year the PLGs were less structured, "which in retrospect was probably a mistake" according to a deputy principal. The teachers did not have enough experience, confidence and guidance in setting their goals and needed structured support to gain experience in developing them. As a consequence, the lead facilitator in the school has run whole-staff and middle-leader meetings to support processes for developing their focuses for TAI. The specialist classroom teacher has gradually taken more responsibility for supporting staff with TAI and the middle leader development associated with this.

The deputy principals thought that actively revisiting inquiry throughout the year (both as a whole staff and within learning areas) was required to sustain teachers' interest and momentum. Initially teachers were encouraged to "just choose a class for TAI" and to "come up with strategies for tracking achievement". In their third year of implementation there is much more of a strategic alliance between students' needs and identifying staff needs to address these students' needs.

There was a resounding accolade for the support from the subject specialist facilitators, who had provided readings and suggestions for inquiry to keep them manageable, kept teachers focused, and linked teachers to people outside the school. Having facilitators to provide advice "on tap" was considered a huge enabler. One of the teachers at this school indicated how the facilitators enabled her development:

> There was 'ongoing learning about how you can do things better' and this led to professional pride and greater job satisfaction. As well there was a 'tyranny of the urgent', somehow having the perspective of the outside [helped]. Having a facilitator … there's accountability [to that person]. I prepared for [the facilitator] because she's coming all the way from Christchurch to see me. (Teacher)

Developmental enablers

The cycles of reflective practice were tied to the school's strategic goals and plans in the second year of implementation. As part of this process, teachers were guided through what would be involved with TAI at whole-staff meetings. However, there were limitations for some teachers associated with this (see the barriers section below), which needed to be managed carefully.

The language of teaching as inquiry took time to evolve because it was infused into the appraisal processes and into some staffroom conversations:

> It's been interesting to see how the conversations have changed in the staffroom. They're asking others 'well, what's working for you?' (Deputy principal)

Although the senior leaders were aware of and used culturally appropriate approaches, especially tikanga during staff meetings, they have identified a need to develop more cultural competencies among the staff and to continue to work on this in the future. There are some promising examples of the use of tikanga in classes, such as the use of a karakia prior to an animal dissection and karakia in the home economics room prior to eating food, as well as the use of te reo Māori as positive feedback responses to students.

The school has provided professional development using examples of small inquiry cycles to illustrate the sorts of things teachers could do. Some teachers realised they could transfer the inquiry process to multiple classes. Teachers acknowledged how it was important for them to be accountable to the senior leaders in the school for implementing TAI, even though some agreed it was what good teachers do anyway. Accountability was reinforced when the school leaders indicated due dates for appraisal goals, gave reminders via email, and set up one-on-one meetings between the deputy principals or HODs with staff. This made it more likely that teachers would reach their goals or consider how their goals might be refined to achieve what they were trying to change.

Achievement enablers

Priority students who were the subject of teachers' inquiry at School B achieved at much higher levels of NCEA (T2) than predicted (T1).

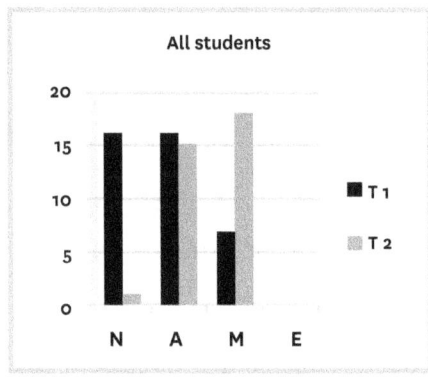
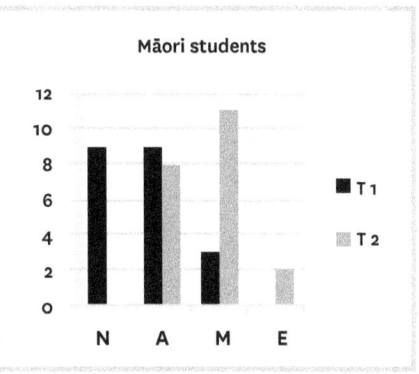

Figure 3: School B: Students' predicted achievement (T1) and actual achievement (T2), in NCEA level 1, 2014

Some of the factors that led to the achievement gains shown in Figure 3 included the support provided by the facilitators (as indicated above), support within staff PLGs, and teachers becoming more aware of their own needs in relation to their students' needs.

Through PLGs teachers focused on particular strategies for teaching and how the information gained when students did these tasks could provide information about changes in students' outcomes. For example, a PLG focused on developing literacy tools to support students' development and wider use of vocabulary. Sharing different examples across learning areas seemed useful as teachers picked up ideas from each other.

In addition, specific literacy tools were developed to target specific student outcomes. For example, a science teacher commented that because the engagement of the girls in her Year 10 science class had not been great, she decided to focus on developing the new science capabilities using the COAL's writing matrix. She commented that students were able to more clearly identify what they needed to work on because of her specific feedback:

> I have been focusing on improving the students' writing. The students really like the feedback I gave using the COAL's sheet as it was quite specific. They could see, for example, that they had the correct ideas but the organisation of their writing needed attention.

As a consequence of this shift in emphasis in teaching, the students' ability to write explanations had improved markedly in this class.

> *"Postponing the summative assessment task until the students had gained the skills was an achievement enabler."*

There was also a shift in terms of how teachers purposefully used formative assessment tasks to provide feedback for improving results in NCEA achievement standards. A science teacher remodeled the way he introduced the first science inquiry achievement standard for his Year 11 science class to provide more structure and stages for feedback during the inquiry processes of planning, conducting, reporting and evaluating the inquiry.

He said that the more structured approach enabled them to experience some success. This gave the students confidence for the rest of the year. Postponing the summative assessment task until the students had gained the skills was an achievement enabler.

Contextual enablers

Members of the senior management conducted a postbox for suggestions at the end of 2012 to initiate the TAI process and to help teachers consider the focus for their inquiry for 2013. In the following year there was an acceptance, among about two-thirds of the teachers, that they would visit each other in their classrooms to provide constructive feedback related to the predetermined goals that each teacher had set. This was quite a shift from what was usual practice at this school.

Other specific strategies that teachers implemented in this school included offering tutorials, one-on-one mentoring during out-of-class hours, and the dean asking the girls at their individual interviews, "What can we do to help you?" The students considered that all of these activities—as well as the way teachers were providing more explicit feedback about their progress—indicated that teachers cared.

Barriers

Initially, when TAI was introduced some staff resisted the idea because they thought what was being proposed was a new way of working and it would add to their workload. They were busy enough and did not see themselves as researchers. They did not understand how it was different to what they were doing already. The senior staff agreed that the way TAI was introduced probably confused some teachers. Indicating that teachers could do "mini" inquiries and sharing specific examples has enabled teachers to consider what is manageable and what focus for their inquiry fits with their targeted planning more directly.

For 2014 the senior management purposefully took a high-trust model for the TAI, whereby staff were given a lot of freedom to choose what they would focus on individually or in groups. One of the deputy principals noted that "some staff chose the path of least resistance" and did not develop clear goals. They really needed more support to develop their goals to keep them focused on the priority learners.

Two-thirds of the way through their second year of implementation the senior leaders estimated that 13 to 14 staff had incorporated TAI as part of routine practice. As a consequence of some teachers taking longer than expected to choose and focus on their goals, the leadership team had to follow up with staff more closely the next year so that goals were set early enough to take action on them.

Also, the school leaders have identified the need to train appraisers for the peer appraisal system across the school. This is so that when teachers visit each other to observe teaching, the conversations are proactive and productive about how to use TAI to help them consider their pedagogical changes. The school leaders commented that there needs to be more clarity about the purpose of any new initiative, otherwise teachers do not see the point in it and there is less chance that they will "buy into it".

Although the specialist classroom teacher role was seen as important, some staff were uncertain about how this role aligned with the TAI initiative. There may be scope within schools to consider how the specialist teacher connects with and works alongside the school liaison facilitator and how they can inform each other about specific teachers' progress. Considering how roles and responsibilities can support and enhance multiple initiatives simultaneously is one of the challenges secondary schools are grappling with. Good communication and networking or sharing ideas could help schools move forward more quickly.

School C

Description of the school

This school is situated in a rural town in the central North Island. It is a state, decile[1] 3 secondary school with a roll of 301 students in 2014. At this time the role consisted of approximately 35 percent Māori, 52 percent NZ European students and about 8 percent students of Samoan descent.

Previously many students chose not to attend this school and opted for other schools in neighbouring towns. This trend was changing, with more students choosing to attend their local high school rather than travel to state schools further away. For example, in 2014

---

1   Deciles are a measure of the socio-economic position of a school's student community relative to other schools throughout the country. For example, decile 1 schools are the 10% of schools with the highest proportion of students from low socio-economic communities, whereas decile 10 schools are the 10% of schools with the lowest proportion of these students. Deciles are used to provide funding to state and state-integrated schools to enable them to overcome the barriers to learning faced by students from lower socio-economic communities. The lower the school's decile, the more funding they receive.

approximately 60 percent of Year 8 students from the area chose to come to School C for Year 9. This was a shift to a total of 91 students in 2014, compared with 65 students in 2013. Clearly the school was doing something right.

The staff at the school had taken on a number of initiatives to help raise the success of their students over the last 5 years. The Secondary Student Achievement project (using TAI) is one of these. In 2014 the school also joined Te Kakahu (a Ministry of Education Building on Success initiative) to enable better connections with iwi. This initiative provided successful connections with key people, and events and encounters for students to connect with members of their Māori community. For example, iwi have assisted with teaching local tikanga to senior Māori students. The intention is that members of the Māori community will further support staff to incorporate and adjust units of work and approaches to teaching to make them more culturally grounded. The school also implemented a new optional course in mātauranga Māori for Year 11–13 students. The staff have noticed that "the kids are standing taller" as a result of these connections with iwi and tikanga Māori.

Leadership

The school principal began at this school in May 2012 and appointed a new deputy principal the following year. There was a very strong vision for the school, driven by the principal. This was underpinned by clear goals for the senior leadership team and staff, which included:

1. raise student engagement and achievement
2. increase excellence in teaching
3. increase the number of students attaining Level 1 NCEA numeracy and literacy
4. raise the percentage of students leaving the school with at least Level 2 NCEA
5. support and increase teachers' use of ICT
6. build a robust appraisal system that supports a culture of inquiry to improve teaching
7. use targeted planning
8. use of TAI—small groups of staff working with a subject expert to focus on priority students' needs.

Making these goals clear and up front was something the principal indicated was very important to her. This, in itself, steered the school with a clear purpose, and was probably very important for getting many staff on board. Not all staff were comfortable with including TAI, and this, along with other reasons, contributed to their decision to leave this school.

The senior leaders in the school were clearly committed to the inquiry process as a means of improving student engagement in schooling and achievement. They were also clear that they were using it as a vehicle for learning at multiple levels: learning and achievement gains for students, teachers learning about their students and being responsive to their needs, teachers learning how to work together to improve outcomes, and school leaders learning how to plan strategically.

TAI as a process linked to teaching was introduced to a small number of staff in 2012. Over the next 3 years there was increasing awareness of the value of TAI for changing teachers' practice as teachers aligned their pedagogies with the learning needs of their students. In the second year of implementation the staff were "buzzing" with ideas and aspects of their teaching they had changed that students also considered made a difference.

The leadership team integrated TAI with the staff appraisal system. This involved teachers collating evidence of changes to their teaching and consequential student outcomes. Like the other two schools profiled earlier, the senior leaders reinforced the idea that this evidence of reflective practice could count for the New Zealand Teachers Council Registered Teacher Criteria. The principal was very clear with staff that all teachers were expected to participate in TAI. The principal also required all departments to submit a report on their progress. Both senior leaders conducted meetings with heads of department about documenting progress with TAI and for student achievement data. This means that the heads of departments were expected to support the process and support their staff inquiries.

As progressively more staff across the school embraced the TAI process they gained confidence in seeking evidence at multiple levels—both their students' and their own successes. The insistence on the mantra "How do you know?" paid off, according to the principal, who indicated that previously there was a lack of rigorous use of data to inform teaching practice or to identify changes that could be made. All of the staff interviewed indicated that there was an emphasis on teaching for better student engagement and better achievement.

The leaders were clear that their role was to get staff excited about doing things differently. They were also very aware of developmental differences among staff, and that some staff needed more support and time to make changes. The principal indicated that if she had not insisted on whole-school changes, they would have lost good teachers due to a perceived lack of direction and leadership.

Focus for inquiry

The school purposefully chose to start TAI as a pilot with a small group of teachers from a range of departments. These teachers focused on how they could meet the needs of a small number of target students. The teachers sought students' voice, including any concerns they had about their learning, in order to identify specific learning needs. Then the teachers developed teaching and learning goals and designed interventions related to these needs.

Part of the planning for TAI involved the teachers reflecting on how they would gain information about student outcomes from everyday class activities. As time passed the teachers became better at collating this information. They shared their inquiry progress and documentation, as part of their appraisal, through the use of a range of templates to record their progress. However, in the first 2 years of implementation there were only a few occasions when teachers shared what they did—and what difference it made to students—with the whole staff. For example, at the end of Term 1 in 2014 they had a 5-minute "ignite" presentation of inquiry outcomes at an all-staff meeting.

The learning area specialists who were supported by Ministry of Education funding provided specific subject-related mentoring. At School C these learning areas were:

- Visual arts (2012/13)
- Health (2012/13)
- Mathematics
- Science
- Social Science.

As part of the school's appraisal system, each staff member was required to develop three goals, for: general progress and achievement, Māori achievement, and personal or professional development. At first many staff found developing their goals difficult because it was time consuming. As they were coached by the school leaders and facilitators, and through seeing examples from some early adopters, they developed more refined skills in creating their inquiry structure and evidence. There was a sense that teachers were developing more realistic goals in the second and third years of implementation than previously, especially goals for Māori students.

The backgrounds of the students who were the focus of the teachers in this school are given in Table 6.

Table 6: Backgrounds of students who were the focus of teachers' inquiries at School C

Number of Māori	Number of Pasifika	Number of ELLs	Number of SEN	Number of students below curriculum level/NCEA	Number of students at curriculum level/NCEA	Number of students above the curriculum level/NCEA
8	3	1	25	32	6	0

Note: ELLs are English Language Learners – these are students who have another language as their first language
SEN are special education needs students

Many of the students who were the focus of teachers' inquiries had special educational needs (SEN) or were not achieving the NCEA level that would be expected for their year level. These criteria were used to identify which students were the priority learners.

Building a community of learners

Although there was a ground-up, student-needs-based focus to the teachers' inquiries about their own teaching, there was also a need to build and share ideas with other teachers who wanted to develop their expertise with a particular emphasis. This focus on students' needs led to the formation of PLGs. Initially these groups supported teachers to come up with goals related to the focus of the PLG. Teachers were able to switch groups if their goals changed. This proved to be very helpful

for some teachers to help them get started. The PLGs focused on:
- literacy apps and Google Docs
- scholarship
- Māori achievement
- managing self
- accelerating learning
- research
- thinking skills
- e-learning.

External drivers

The declining school role over many years prior to the appointment of the current principal was an incentive for the school to work differently. Attracting students to come to the school was very important to rebuild its reputation and to provide education for the people of its community. The principal was clear in communicating the moral purpose of improving students' outcomes, both with her staff and with the community. She was determined to change the way the school was perceived, and she knew from her work with the Education Review Office that it was very important to connect with the school community.

There were also many opportunities for the students to feel welcomed and valued as part of this repositioning of the school, which has led students to develop a sense of belonging, whereby they consider that staff care about them and their progress.

The staff were reminded about the key findings for effective teaching of Māori children (Bishop & Berryman, 2012), such as the importance of positive relationships and interactions between teachers and students and having high expectations for achievement. They discussed how teachers can make a difference by managing learning that incorporates interactive experiences between teachers and students, who reflect together about their ongoing achievement

The principal appointed a deputy principal to drive teaching and learning across the school and to oversee the school's professional appraisal system, among other responsibilities. He actively participates in TAI because he feels it is important to model the practices he expects of the teachers.

Staff at this school identified that they had to raise achievement, especially in literacy and numeracy. As indicated in Table 6, many students at this school had special educational needs that had to be accommodated. There was also a need to raise NCEA scores and underachievement of Māori, Pasifika and ELL learners. Table 7 shows the data for students' achievement in NCEA in Levels 1 and 2 in 2012 and 2013.

Table 7: The percentage of students at School C achieving Level 1 and Level 2 NCEA, 2012 and 2013

		Percentage with NCEA Level 1 or above		Percentage with NCEA Level 2 or above	
		2012	2013	2012	2013
Māori	Total	37.5	66.7	16.7	58.3
Pasifika	Total	x	87.5	x	50
NZ European/ Pākehā	Total	89.5	83	75.4	70.2

There is a marked increase in the percentage of Māori and Pasifika students at this school who achieved NCEA at both levels from 2012 to 2013.

Further analysis of the levels of achievement in NCEA are shown in Figure 4. This data represents Time 1 and Time 2 for the students at School C. Time 1 data is the average predicted achievement of students, and Time 2 data is the actual achievement in NCEA.

Figure 4: Numbers of students and their predicted achievement (T1) and their actual achievement in NCEA Level 1 (T2), School C for 2014.

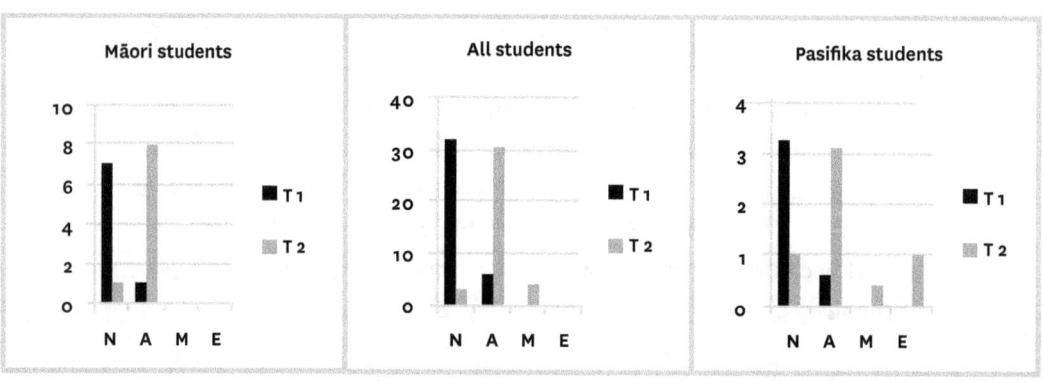

The achievement shown in Figure 4 indicates that there was improved success in the levels of NCEA outcomes for Māori and Pasifika students. This is indicated by both a decrease in the number of students who did not achieve (N), and a slight increase in the number who moved to Merit (M) and Excellence grades (E) in NCEA standards assessments.

Structural and procedural enablers

There were many structural and procedural enablers that supported this school on its journey with TAI. These included Ministry support in the form of subject-specific facilitators, the PLGs and departmental meetings.

Ministry of Education funding and support of the facilitators provided a significant boost to the schools' progress. The facilitators offered regular support, checking in with teachers in person and online, yet challenged the teachers to move forward and try new ideas in their teaching, particularly using literacy tools. The facilitators maintained contact with the teachers through email and provided suggestions and questions from a distance, as well as face to face.

Most PLG groups met weekly during 2013 and 2014. The school provided time for these meetings as part of the school day. At these meetings, as well as more informally, teachers shared ideas and collaborated with others within PLGs. These opportunities were highly valued by the teachers and the leaders, who agreed there had been huge development in the discussions at the PLGs. This seemed to help teachers to develop their goals more easily.

Pairs of teachers in the same subject area or whole departments were meeting together regularly to discuss and reflect on their TAI focus. Often they were pleasantly surprised at the kinds of things they learnt from each other. The board of trustees has been kept informed of changes and successes through the principals' reports. A staff member presented her inquiry and findings to the board at the end of 2013, and there have also been several opportunities to convey changes at the school to the community.

Developmental enablers

The developmental enablers related to aspects of TAI were modified over time. One was the ongoing clarification of what TAI is and what teachers could do differently to reflect and evaluate the outcomes to inform their teaching. Other developmental shifts related to how teachers worked more collaboratively with the facilitators over time and within their PLG groups to support each other's development. This was especially the case for rethinking what assessments might be offered and students' readiness to sit formal assessments.[2]

Staff considered there was a clear direction and purpose for engaging in TAI at their school. They thought that their mini inquiries into their teaching were "what good teachers should be doing anyway". Many of them agreed that the TAI process "made it more formal" but also enabled them to extend the types of experiences they provided students For example, they have been pleased to be able to take students on trips, develop internship approaches (in home economics) and create new digital activities to stimulate students' interests.

Some teachers celebrated the creative elements of this type of professional learning. It gave them impetus and a reason for trying new ideas. Three teachers commented in different contexts that they appreciated the creative aspects and flexibility in what they could try out. One of the teachers said that having choice was "somewhat motivating". He said that he had "actually been given a free hand" to do what he wanted and he was backed up by the leadership team "to go for it". Because teachers chose their own focus for TAI, the deputy principal had noticed less "eye rolling" during staff meetings and increased teacher engagement: "There is less watching the clock" and "teachers are staying longer in the staffroom to discuss their ideas". The development of teachers' thinking such that they believe they can be agents of their own professional learning because they are supported is developing well in this school.

From all the staff we spoke to there was a sense of teaching as learning, and that self-questioning what they do and why they do it was now a core part of their work. When teachers considered how effective their changes were they asked themselves why activities might have worked or not worked and in what ways they worked in order to

---

[2] The New Zealand education system allows schools to choose what assessments they can offer students. Therefore the interpretation of the assessment system is in itself an enabler for freeing up teachers' thinking about what they cover in classes.

identify success factors. However, not all teachers saw this professional learning aspect straight away. One teacher stated that initially she just didn't "get it". She heard several accounts in staff meetings and worked collegially in her PLG, but she "still didn't get it". She attributed this to the way it was introduced, as if it was something new, rather than what good teachers would be doing anyway. She had been grappling with trying to work out how she could use data to inform her teaching. The realisation that any student outcomes, such as completed student activities or observations of attitudinal changes in students, could be used as data helped her to understand what she could do.

One of the key development enablers was how, over time, the facilitators worked more collaboratively with the teachers to help them reconsider the subject-specific understanding of the language used for NCEA assessment tasks. As part of this development in teacher thinking (i.e. that either students didn't understand subject-related concepts or the subject-specific language, or were not able to do what was required in the assessment task), they realised that they needed to take more time to unpack each assessment and make sure students were well prepared prior to completing the tasks. This has meant that some departments are offering fewer NCEA credits to enable them to increase their emphasis on quality teaching rather than quantity of assessments. The teachers reported that as a consequence the students are assessed when they are ready, rather than according to a predetermined timetable or scheduling of units of work. This represents a fundamental shift in teacher thinking about the needs of students.

A change in both types of standards and in the number of credits offered in subject domains for students in the senior school helped to retain some students who would otherwise have left. For example, hospitality has been introduced as a new subject in the school, providing the opportunity for students to gain industry qualifications. The staff viewed this addition very positively because it enabled students to link learning at school directly with employment possibilities, and therefore increased student engagement.

Some of the PLGs purposefully developed tools to support the staff to use in different subject areas. For example, the e-learning PLG in this school also supported staff skill development by collaboratively developing learning tools for students. Also, the teachers developed their own digital dashboards[3] to share work among the PLG and as a means to provide feedback electronically to students.

Several staff discussed the importance of connecting with students outside of class time because it made a difference and helped to build positive relationships with students. These "chats in the playground" were described by one staff member as being crucial to figuring out what students were interested in, and perhaps what issues the students were currently grappling with at home or elsewhere. The facilitators said that they often talked with teachers about "place-based contexts" to increase student engagement and to support student learning, as research on learning indicates that more effective retention occurs when the context is familiar to students (Bransford, Brown, & Cocking, 1999).

Achievement enablers
Several staff talked about the buzz they got when they tried something new and it worked. At first it was difficult for them to use subjective elements of student progress. However, student engagement was measured across the school through attendance data, and this showed a marked improvement in successive years. We also provide some examples below of where teachers noticed changes in students' behaviour across a range of subjects.

A geography facilitator produced a success story of a student for whom English was a second language to illustrate changes in achievement for this student over successive years.

Success story: Social science facilitator
A Fijian student spoke about her strong interest in the contexts used in geography and that the teaching and learning strategies were engaging. She made a specific comment about the feedback given in her learning log, saying that the teacher really cared about her and her learning. By the end of the 1st year this student believed that she could achieve and had the ability to do so. She spoke of her love for geography, feeling motivated by the contexts offered, and appreciated the individualised attention. Her teacher gave her leadership roles in class, which the student saw as a privilege and that there were high

---

3 Digital dashboards are a visual collection and representation of learning support tools and devices that can also provide summaries of learning progress.

expectations that she aspired to. This student gained an endorsement in NCEA with Merit at Level 2, and went on to gain Scholarship geography. The teacher considered that the student would not have achieved a Scholarship without this level of positive support.

Other examples of success stories related to teachers identifying particular ways in which they changed how they related to students, or changed the teaching and learning activities to better meet the specific and targeted needs of their learners. For example, the two home room teachers reported that they constantly analysed data from asTTle engagement measures, attendance records, attitude and task avoidance monitoring, etc. The school was using the AVAILLL reading programme and designated the last class of the day as "sustained silent reading" time. One teacher observed that in the previous year many students would page flick quickly and "pretend" to be reading. This year students had wanted to get books out of the library, and one of the reluctant readers even asked if she could read out loud to the class—much to the amazement of the teacher, because previously this student had been a very reluctant reader.

Through the TAI process the PE teacher at School C decided to delve deeper into why her students were not getting NZQA Scholarships at Year 13. She reviewed and changed her units of work in response to her observations when visiting another school, where the students were getting Scholarships. Since making these changes, two of her PE students gained Scholarships in 2013. She considered that these students would not have got Scholarships if she had not made these changes to guided and structured approaches to learning PE concepts.

The science department discussed how they tracked the achievement of students topic by topic. Science staff indicated that the Year 9 students caught the "inquisitive bug" and were asking more questions than previously. Teachers were noticing that students wanted to come to class and seemed disappointed when they said on the playground to the teacher, "Oh [sigh!] we don't have science today". The teachers were pleased with the students' increased motivation.

Contextual enablers

A transition point for this school was getting a new principal who was committed to professional learning and relentless effort to improve outcomes for students. Twenty-three percent of staff have moved on since her arrival. The principal admitted that new staff could be persuaded more easily to take on shared goals and philosophies.

Some structural changes enabled subjects to be combined. For example, a Year 9 social science class has been combined with a digital technology class. According to the teachers, the students perceived that there was a seamless transition between these subjects because they were blended. The results in social science for these students have "been exceptional" because they see inquiry and the use of technology as synonymous. Staff indicated that most students now have the attitude that "if you don't turn up you might miss something." An example was given of a girl who, although she was attending a funeral, phoned in to connect with her group to join in the discussion with them during class because she wanted to contribute her ideas.

The teachers were now considering different ways of enabling learning, and they had gained a sense of freedom so that it was "OK to try things out" and "that if it didn't work out then we have to think about why". For example, there was some experimentation with the use of Google Docs, where students created works and published them online. This did not happen previously. Feedback from teachers to students and students to teachers was also better enabled through the use of Google Docs. A positive outcome was that some of the teachers were seeking daily feedback from the students about what they had done in each lesson.

Many members of staff indicated that everyday talk in the staffroom had changed from "pathologising" about what was wrong with the students to talk about their own teaching: what they have done and how it is making a difference. Teachers felt they were discussing students and their backgrounds more often so that they had a better understanding of each student and their motivations. As one teacher said, "We are talking about things that matter".

Collegiality was perceived to have increased at multiple levels. This included between inquiry partners (where two teachers were working collaboratively on an initiative or change to teaching), within the PLGs and at a whole-school level. There is scope to develop collaboration and sharing of successes further.

Several staff mentioned that since participating in TAI they were more aware of what helps students to learn. They commented that often students just needed to eat and that they let them eat in class, even though they were aware of the school rules about this. They reported that letting students eat in class had made a difference to their readiness to learn.

In the end-of-year survey (2014) about TAI and about PLGs in general, 28 out of 30 staff were overwhelmingly positive and enjoyed the processes currently in place. As a result, TAI will continue in a similar format in this school.

Barriers

Several teachers and both school leaders agreed that it probably takes more than 2 years to get all teachers to a point where they feel comfortable developing their goals, implementing their inquiry cycles, considering the effectiveness of what they have done and reporting to others. The accountability for doing so was augmented by the visits and emails from the facilitators, who, according to one teacher "have got this lovely way of being assertive". The facilitators were seen to be the ones who asked the hard questions and played the role of provocateur. At the same time, they were viewed as being supportive by listening and providing valuable suggestions for next steps.

Other teachers mentioned that they would like to do more of some things but they do not have enough time in class so they have to prioritise their time. For example, the two home-room teachers discussed how they would like to be more thorough in developing individual education programmes for each student. It required time and space to leave the other students to get on with tasks while the teachers worked one on one with students, and often students in their classes were not able to work independently. "Time is worth everything", one teacher commented indicating how precious time was and the need to use time effectively. Therefore they wanted to make meetings count for something and to contribute to their progress. Some teachers wanted to be more innovative and creative in the use of e-learning tools and strategies with students and often had to use their own time to do this.

Initially there was a focus on hard data as evidence of shifts in students' outcomes. Gathering data related to a small shift in students' learning behaviour and engagement was not always possible. Sometimes the difference a teacher makes takes developmental time, and the evidence is not always immediately obvious. As well, the way in which data is gathered seems to be important. For example, the homeroom teachers commented that there is a huge difference in results when some students undertake the paper asTTle tests compared with online e-asTTle tests, and this is a source of interest to them. The common tests for Years 9 and 10 across the core subjects potentially enable comparisons across classes using the same tool. However, this was seen as constraining teachers' creativity, especially when working with students who needed more literacy or numeracy support. The common tests may not be appropriate as a measure of achievement change, especially for special needs students, since there are other measures (e.g. asTTle) that may provide better indications of progress. One teacher commented that there was therefore incongruence between "what you'd like to teach and what you're required to report on."

Writing down reflections was considered a barrier for one teacher, who indicated she would rather record her thoughts into a dictaphone. She thought this would take less time and she could do it more immediately—when she had the thoughts, rather than having to make a special time to write in a diary or "fill in the forms". Several teachers mentioned that filling in templates or forms for establishing TAI put them off initially. For some this was because they had not made the connection between how using the forms to direct their inquiries could support student gains. Therefore, making clear the purpose of using templates was important. Although the deputy principal provided a range of templates to record TAI processes, some staff would have liked other ways to record their progress—such as audio recording.

The size of the school and access to subject specialist expertise could be considered a limiting factor for ongoing sustainability. Teachers were just starting to look beyond the school and to use subject associations or colleagues in neighbouring schools for additional support. They have since been supported to do this through regional cluster meetings during the year. Despite this, the small school size has meant that it has been easier to implement a whole-school approach for TAI.

Teachers mentioned that "we don't know what we don't know" and thought that there could be a mechanism to give them access to online research papers and more readings. The staff wanted access to what other teachers and researchers have found previously. They indicated that the school library did a good job as far as providing resources for the students, but as researchers of their own practice they needed access to educational research literature. They appreciated the recommended readings that the facilitators provided. The specialist classroom teacher has recently established an online Google site to enable readings and research to be shared with staff.

Summary

Teachers in the case study schools indicated that TAI was successful because of a number of structural, procedural and achievement enablers. One of the most significant was the funded subject-specific facilitators' support and their ongoing communication about aspects to consider. Timperley (2011b) has also indicated the importance of external facilitation that builds capabilities for professional and organisational adaptive expertise. All of the teachers interviewed indicated that they would not have been able to carry out their inquiry independently without the support of facilitators in the first 2 years.

The facilitated support enabled the teachers to undertake TAI, which consequently shifted their beliefs about priority learners, such as their backgrounds, prior knowledge and capabilities, and what their needs were for the next steps in learning. Many examples were cited by the teachers in these schools about how their priority learners, in particular, had become more engaged and curious about their subjects and their learning because the teachers had focused on their students' specific needs, which were often discipline specific.

The teachers indicated that they were becoming more familiar with a range of pedagogies to support Māori and Pasifika students, learners with special education needs, learners from low socioeconomic backgrounds and English-language learners (ELLs). They were developing adaptive expertise and inquiry approaches to teaching, which were based on their students' needs. Initially they had difficulty figuring out specific literacy challenges and assessment challenges. However, by incorporating subject-based language support activities as well as customising their activities and resources, they saw changes in students' behaviours (increased motivation) and achievement. An intense focus such as this can be quite time consuming, but is an emphasis of *The New Zealand Curriculum* that is starting to gain wider application.

The teachers experienced the value of sharing how changes in emphasis on subject-specific literacy and ICT strategies supported learning. The culture of a learning community was progressing in all three schools because the teachers, leaders and facilitators were becoming clearer about their goals and the outcomes they wanted, and how these exemplify either teacher or student success. However, these processes take time.

> *"Because senior leaders were seen to be making an effort to create more time, there are strong indications, in all three case study schools, that more teachers are willing to be involved."*

As Stoll, Fink and Earl (2003) have discussed at length, time to meet with facilitators or groups of other staff, time to discuss, time to read and discuss research, time to reflect and plan next steps in teaching, and time to evaluate what worked and what could be refined were very important in the schools they worked in. This also applied to teachers in our case study schools. The leaders were very aware of these needs and sought ways to make more time available as a resource for TAI. This often involved gaining efficiencies; for example, some meeting agendas were shortened and notices were sent out by email; clearer purposes for meetings with goals or outlines helped everyone to focus and proceed much more quickly; and some teachers' timetables were synchronised, where possible. Because senior leaders were seen to be making an effort to create more time, there are strong indications, in all three case study schools, that more teachers are willing to be involved.

As a result of their participation in the Secondary Student Achievement project, teachers and school leaders noted that their enthusiasm for teaching had been rekindled, boredom had been averted, and they were finding ways to increase their teaching competencies. More explicit ways of sharing these discoveries should be a focus for the future.

In addition to the subject specialist facilitation support, the conditions for the successful use of TAI for professional learning and improving outcomes included:

- teachers understanding that small changes in their teaching can bring about positive change in student engagement and intellectual curiosity, and consequently outcomes, but not all changes will bring about immediate changes to measurable outcomes
- support for teachers (from facilitators, each other and senior leadership) to develop in-depth reflection, which required prioritising tasks and events and having opportunities to discuss ideas without fear of judgement
- in-depth reflection, which required teachers to identify ways to value students, and use student voice and feedback to inform next steps in teaching, and realising there are multiple ways to get this information
- the skills required for in-depth reflection, which required time to develop and time for reflection and sharing
- whole-school policy and strategic changes, such as linking TAI plans and outcomes to the school's appraisal system, which supported the development of a culture of continuous teaching improvement for improving student outcomes.

Guiding questions

1. What key idea from these case studies could you apply to your teaching?
2. How do you know if your students are motivated to learn? What indicators might you look for?
3. Can you provide an example of how you use student voice to inform your teaching?
4. What tools might be useful for you to reflect on your teaching?
5. What structural aspects of your school or centre might need to change to provide more time for teachers to undertake TAI?
6. How can TAI be managed within busy teachers' workdays?

Chapter 4: Influences on pedagogical development

In this chapter the role of the subject-specific facilitated support and other crucial aspects related to the implementation of TAI across all the schools in the project are discussed. These aspects relate to the support processes for TAI and how the culture of continuous improvement was promoted within the schools. In-depth TAI that focused on four to five learners structured the TAI process to make it specific, rather than a more general inquiry approach that tries to address multiple and complex issues for whole classes. The subject-specialist facilitators provided the main support for this form of TAI.

The role of the facilitators

The focus for all teachers in this initiative was to increase the engagement and achievement of their priority learners. The facilitators provided mentoring and pedagogical approaches that helped teachers identify the students' needs within a specific subject and level taught. The focus on students' needs in relation to learning specific content was very important, because the teachers wanted fresh input and ideas about what they could try out to support students' learning. They were pragmatic in that they wanted to implement specific teaching activities that would target key content or key learning processes, such as improving students' literacy or understanding of assessment requirements in their specific learning area.

As well as providing subject-specific tasks, all facilitators had one-on-one conversations with teachers about what it meant to be culturally responsive and the need to identify what their students were interested in. Levin (2003) has commented that often teachers need these conversations with knowledgeable others:

> Teachers can continue to develop their thinking about pedagogy when they interact with others to get needed support. This includes support from family, friends, colleagues or mentors. (p. 277)

As shown in the success stories throughout this book and the case study summaries in Chapter 3, the facilitators supported TAI that enabled the teachers to change their beliefs about their priority learners; that is, the students' prior knowledge and capabilities, and what their needs were for next steps in learning.

The facilitators established the importance of stretching students' potential. This went beyond raising expectations about what students could do: it included identifying experiences that were relevant to the students in terms of their language needs, as suggested for raising Pasifika literacy by Fletcher, Parkhill and Fa'afoi (2005). As a consequence, teaching behaviours changed in relation to developing new activities, and teachers gave more positive, timely and high-quality feedback to students. In one case study school, the feedback was almost immediate—through the use of Google Docs.

In all three case study schools—and many in the wider project—the use of formative assessment supported the development of both students' and teachers' knowledge about learning progressions, especially in the case of identifying the reading challenges for ELLs. One of the examples from the international language teacher's comments illustrates this, as reading a foreign language was a key focus for her priority learners:

> I have been able to practically implement the strategies with most of the reading that we do in class. I am more aware of a variety of strategies to use, so I can vary these. The girls enjoy being part of this inquiry and are pleased with our interest in their learning. The girls enjoy verbalising the process of their reading/learning. (Language teacher)

The regular face-to-face meetings between facilitators and teachers undertaking TAI were supplemented with emails and the use of

Google Docs, where readings could be uploaded and shared with a range of teachers. Teachers also uploaded documents to their Google folders, and these were often visible to other teachers teaching in the same subject area. This was a very supportive aspect for the teachers, who realised they could learn a lot from each other, and even the teachers who were very experienced commented that sharing ideas helped them to consider ideas they might try.

A facilitator success story indicated how teachers incorporated the advice and suggestions that facilitators gave and then reflected on what effect this had on students.

Success story: Facilitator

A teacher was concerned that her students' note taking from readings was muddled and produced little sustained learning. We suggested the students could develop a system for marking the texts they read as they read them. Following our example, the teacher modelled [a text annotation process] [out loud] for the students. They used a range of ways to indicate significant ideas or features in the texts such as highlighting, underlining, shading, boxing out, circling and numbering. The students also used a purpose-designed graphic organiser to gather and sort the marked information in the readings. The students indicated that these processes helped them to take notes much more clearly than previously. Using graphic organisers made it more straightforward for students to transfer their gathered knowledge to a prose explanation. The graphic organisers also served as checklists as they wrote. Undertaken in this way, note-taking became much more focused. It provided a way to undertake a deep and critical reading, associated with a thinking exercise that required selection and organisation, and finally an activity, which supported writing development.

Teachers often considered their students' literacy learning needs and questioned their teaching practices that currently supported—or did not support—these needs. Then the evidence of student outcomes was used: usually the outcomes or artifacts that students generated from a particular learning activity. Teachers could then gauge whether the changes made a difference for their students or not. This evidence was a prime motivator for making future changes to their practice. However, sometimes the teachers did not know about specific strategies or the kinds of changes they could make to help address students' needs. This is why connecting with others who may 'seed' ideas was so important. Teachers were supported to identify what they needed in terms of their professional learning related to their students' needs.

One of the science facilitators commented that it was very important for her to find out more about the strengths of the teachers she was working with and help them to identify their professional and resource needs:

> Teachers who are open to sharing information about themselves and their practice have helped me appreciate how much better I can support teachers with the TAI cycle when I really know the teacher. Conversations in the workplace have also enabled changes to be made to my facilitator practice. I have learned to dig deep to find the strengths and areas of need of teachers and, most importantly, ask challenging questions. It is essential to challenge teachers' assumptions if they are to make changes to their practice to improve outcomes for their priority students.

As this facilitator indicated, knowing the teachers was important. Therefore a longer-term relationship supported both the teachers' development and the way in which the facilitator worked with her teachers. It is not easy to challenge your own or others' assumptions about teaching. Sometimes teachers needed a significant other person—in this case a facilitator—to help identify what underlying assumptions led to choosing approaches to teaching and the consequent experiences given to students. Teachers and facilitators asked questions such as "How did you know that might work for your students?" or "What have you tried already and how did that support your priority learners in particular?"

The liaison facilitator for School B indicated that her work in 2015 has extended to consider a faded guidance approach to help enable leadership within the school to sustain TAI in the longer term:

> As the liaison facilitator in School B, I brought the middle leaders together once a term during the first year of this co-ordinating role, to share their TAI. The second year, after modelling such a meeting for the DP in term 1, the DP conducted the meetings, with [me] the facilitator only providing minimal guidelines. This has been an intentional strategy to develop leadership capacity and sustainability.

Guidance from those supporting the school was gradually withdrawn to enable the school leaders to take on more responsibility for whole-school development. The amount of fading depended on the confidence of teachers and leaders to take on the leadership of TAI and to take risks.

The teachers who undertook the inquiry cycles in the case study schools were supported by many people, including PLD facilitators. There was reasonable consensus among the teachers about how the facilitators had worked in collaboration with them. Working alongside teachers to develop their practice in relation to specific students' needs was the mode of operation, rather than telling teachers what to do or providing solutions. In other words, the facilitation of the TAI process was collaborative, using a peer collegial approach *with* teachers in order to empower them to make decisions, rather than professional development that was *done to* teachers.

Being willing to make changes, and being flexible

One of the things that struck us about the teachers who agreed to be in the first trial groups for TAI in these schools was their general willingness to try out new ways of teaching. A sense of being comfortable with risk taking seemed to be important. These teachers also knew it was important to take action because it was, after all, their students' future achievement at stake. As Timperley et al. (2014) indicated:

> In a truly transformational learning system, the focus is on high quality and high equity for every learner, regardless of their starting point. In our transformed schools, every learner will cross the stage with dignity, purpose and options. In addition, learners will leave our schools and other learning settings *more* curious than when they arrived. (p. 3)

While the outcomes have been clearly stated, Timperley et al. go on to say that "how we transform schools is less succinct" or in other words, the processes for enabling transformation are not as clearly defined. There are multiple strategies for improving quality and equity. The decisions about which strategies are appropriate and can be implemented will depend on context, including the human resources and how these can be leveraged for the best possible outcomes.

It seems that often when changes are implemented there is both a developmental aspect, in terms of identifying changes that will make a difference for students, as well as a knowledge component, in terms of what and how those changes can be made to pedagogy. For this reason the project took into account previous findings about curriculum implementation in New Zealand.

For example, in their review of curriculum implementation, Cowie, Hipkins, Keown and Boyd (2011) indicated that teachers were keen to trial new ideas after a professional learning encounter, but many teachers often quickly reverted to their previous ways of teaching, possibly through inertia or lack of ongoing support. Cowie et al. argued that teachers need time and space to be able to discuss the exemplars, create their own activities and trial them with their classes. It was reported that teachers also needed appropriate skills to provide quality feedback, guidance and encouragement to students, and to share these ideas with other teachers. Internationally, the most successful professional development models have been identified as having ongoing, longer-term, iterative, discursive and reflective components built in (Darling-Hammond, Wei, Andree, Richardson, & Orphanos, 2009; Loucks-Horsley, Stiles, Mundry, Love, & Hewson, 2010).

Our experience in this project over 3 years has indicated that where teachers were relentlessly curious about the effects of their teaching, and when they applied this curiosity directly to the needs of their students and then sought creative possibilities, they were more likely to be successful in turning around outcomes for students. This also required them to seek constant feedback from students about whether the changes were making a difference for them. Teachers often found that students previously had not been as attuned to thinking about how different types of learning experiences might affect the way they learn. Therefore, working with feedback loops and using these to seek and consider creative solutions was important.

At a whole-school level, in terms of supporting the use and understanding of TAI, the school leaders and the facilitators had to be flexible and reflect on the progress of groups of staff. The ultimate goal was to improve student outcomes and teaching approaches that would achieve this, but the pathway to get more teachers on board was not always clear.

Developing and using feedback loops

One of the characteristics of the leadership teams in the case study schools was their ability to be flexible about how TAI might be implemented as it progressed. They were also willing to learn. This was very important, because checking in with middle leaders and staff about progress indicated those aspects that needed more attention or that needed rethinking or refining.

An example of this was in School B in the first year of implementation. The deputy principal provided structured forms for teachers to use to develop their inquiry projects. He knew that some teachers needed a structure to help them get started and therefore provided a tool to help teachers develop their focus and reflect on their progress with TAI. However, many teachers found this structure too constraining. Fortunately they fed back their opinion and discussed alternative strategies for reflecting on their teaching (e.g. using a cellphone or dictaphone to record their thinking and submitting sound files). This, they indicated, would make them more willing to participate and allowed for flexible options for recording their professional progress with implementing TAI.

Feedback loops also enabled groups of teachers to consider how they could target and develop their TAI "adventures". A literacy facilitator described in a success story how, through his work with a school over several years, he was able to identify strategies that might be useful for whole-school literacy development. He made recommendations about running seminars within and across departments and setting up leadership teams. These ideas were subsequently used over 2 successive years. (More details about the specific strategies they used are provided in Chapter 5.) The openness and willingness of leaders to listen to alternative possibilities for how TAI might work, and the realisation that this may need to be flexible to accommodate the different needs of teachers, enabled whole-school processes to progress and be modified or refined over successive years. The leaders were not precious about the way in which TAI should be implemented.

Keeping perspective

At first most of the teachers found it quite difficult to identify a focus for their inquiry. This varied in the schools depending on how TAI was introduced and how confident teachers were with getting evidence of changes in learning. Constructing a question to drive TAI became easier when teachers looked at student achievement information or asked students directly, "What are you good at?" and "What do you need help with?" An initial focus on interest groups through PLGs provided teachers with shared ideas that could be considered across groups of teachers, but these were not necessarily directly related to the individual needs of their students. As a result, some teachers got confused between the agendas of the PLGs and what their students' needed. However, once they identified which students they would work with and what these priority learners needed, their TAI took a leap forward.

Some examples in Chapters 2 and 3 showed how small changes to teaching led to improved student outcomes. Choosing four to five students seemed to be manageable in terms of focus. Often the question that was first developed was changed or refined when teachers found out more about their students or observed how they were or were not using tools, or not grasping key ideas well.

Transfer of pedagogical understanding among teachers was enabled in this project in a number of ways. Firstly, ideas for TAI were shared among pairs of teachers in the same subject areas and among members of PLGs. Secondly, in smaller schools the priority learners that teachers identified were often the same as those identified by their colleagues in other subject areas. Therefore, when cross-subject area groups met, there was some transfer of knowledge about specific learners. This provided opportunities for useful information through feedback loops about how learners were responding to different sorts of emphases in different subjects.

Often teachers identified that their priority learners had multiple needs. Potentially there were multiple ways to address these needs, which meant teachers had to make choices about what might work best for each student. The dilemma is in knowing how the changes make a difference for students. In School B, an example of a teacher's story about how she worked individually with a reluctant student illustrates how she tried multiple strategies by connecting with topics of interest for the student and working specifically with the student on developing her skills.

Success story: History teacher

My most successful target student this year is FS, a Māori female, who has a very low level of self-confidence and most of the time believes that "an academic subject" is out of her league. She is also frequently absent from school and lacks motivation. After eight lessons with me the girl approached her dean and requested to be removed from history, as she found my expectations, the volume of class work and homework "outrageously high," and wanted to have "an easy option."

I was sure I could make her work and spoke to the dean and requested that FS stay with me. I started working one-on-one with her, helping her with her first internal achievement standard. I gave her the opportunity to choose her own inquiry topic and she felt extremely happy, and in a way special, that I consulted her and gave her the freedom to choose the research topic and find something that she is interested in. She began to come to my lunchtime tutorials because I told her that if she wanted to finish it she needed to spend extra time with me. FS completed the first assessment with a Merit grade, and she started attending every single tutorial (four times per week) in order to prepare and pass the second internal. She completed it with another Merit grade and then finished the third one with an Achieved grade, as she was away from school for quite some time and could not attend my tutorials. However, it seemed that my constant encouragement, extra one-on-one time, and persistence made the required shift, and now FS got 3rd in the History class [overall]. She is entered in two external standards and is currently working hard to prepare herself for them.

Teachers found that the skills each student needed could be quite different. Sometimes, as in the science teacher's success story from School A in Chapter 2, they were surprised that the interventions they had tried in their first year of TAI did not always work with different students in their second year. Therein lies the challenge when working with and targeting specific individual differences: different activities and strategies may be required to address the same issue. Sometimes teachers found it a dilemma to know which skills to focus on. In the end, they either went ahead and just picked one, got advice from their facilitator or asked the students what they would like to start with.

Sometimes their focus related to students' understanding of what was required in assessments for gaining a pass or higher grades.

At times the facilitators reminded the teachers about the focus of *The New Zealand Curriculum* and its aspirations. This especially applied to the use of TAI, and how changing assessment practices as part of broader pedagogical change can make a difference for students. The *Curriculum* advises in the section on assessment:

> The primary purpose of assessment is to improve students' learning and teachers' teaching as both student and teacher respond to the information that it provides. With this in mind, schools need to consider how they will gather, analyse, and use assessment information so that it is effective in meeting this purpose. Assessment for the purpose of improving student learning is best understood as an ongoing process that arises out of the interaction between teaching and learning. It involves the focused and timely gathering, analysis, interpretation, and use of information that can provide evidence of student progress. Much of this evidence is 'of the moment'. Analysis and interpretation often take place in the mind of the teacher, who then uses the insights gained to shape their actions as they continue to work with their students. (Ministry of Education, 2007, p. 39)

Across many of the schools and subject areas involved in the wider project, keeping a focus on 'How do you know?' in relation to formative assessment outcomes was very important. One of the most important changes to pedagogy was in how teachers used everyday activities to scan and search for how well students were achieving and what skills the gaps in progress signified. In this way they gained information about students' progress. This was a key shift in informing teachers' planning and inquiry processes.

Summary

There were many influences on the pedagogical development of teachers, but in this model teachers' needs were driven by the needs of their focus students. The subject specialist facilitators supported individuals and groups of teachers to identify what their priority learners needed. Then they made suggestions or helped teachers to develop tasks to address the specific needs of the focus learners. They also had discussions with teachers about how they would know if the changes had been successful.

Facilitators also made suggestions to school leaders about applying what teachers were learning in one subject to another subject. Some schools found that the changes in pedagogy fell broadly under the banner of specific content and skills related to their subject, developing students' literacy (subject-specific vocabulary, text discriminating and writing tasks), as well as specific ways to unpick the assessment requirements for their subject.

Guiding questions

1. How do you use information related to the learning of your students to help you to identify your own professional learning needs?
2. Can you give an example of where you have used a formative task to find out what you need to focus on more in your teaching?
3. How can you identify why students are not achieving? What tools have you used?
4. Students' needs can vary significantly. Can you provide an example of where you designed a teaching activity for the diverse needs of learners, or that catered for a range of outcomes?

Chapter 5: Developing a learning community

Supporting the team
Effective group learning among teachers tends to require plenty of opportunities for dialogue, observation and reflection, mutual trust, and multiple attempts to change without fear of judgement or failure (Kaser & Halbert, 2014). This is because changes in teaching rarely have immediate and obvious effects on student outcomes. The team support and team reflection in all case study schools was not always obvious to the teachers, especially in the 1st year of implementation. Our discussions with the leaders in these schools signaled that they knew their support and commitment to TAI was a key ingredient to its implementation and acceptance as part of their school's professional learning culture. They also knew that it was their role to provide coherence, and to make connections between staff, ideas and other things happening in the school.

Previously, all of our case study schools had whole-school emphases on professional learning. Rightly so, this has generally been targeted at general needs that have been identified over larger groups of students. In many schools, students have specific needs related to literacy development. Therefore it was not uncommon for schools to have focused on literacy professional learning for all of the staff.

For example, in one of the schools participating in the wider

Secondary Student Achievement project, the literacy specialist facilitator noted in a success story how a principal he worked with embraced the idea that he had to lead the school with TAI and chose to emphasise the importance of literacy development across the whole school.

Success story: Literacy specialist

I was quickly impressed by the principal's involvement and his clear determination that this professional learning [PL] was to be the primary focus of school-wide PL during this time. He attended every lead-group PL session; sought to discuss the learning with members of the lead team; and regularly visited classes to see how aspects of the learning were being put into practice. When talking to the staff as a whole, he regularly referred to the literacy PL programme or some particular illustration of it in action. The awareness he so gained through his active participation led him to have the Board grant additional non-teaching time during the school day to the literacy leader [himself a faculty head] so that he could mentor his fellow lead-team members, visit them in their classes, model literacy learning activities for them, and regularly reflect with the lead team on the experience of what everyone was learning.

Clearly, senior leaders have a role in setting the tone and direction for implementing TAI and providing resources, as appropriate, to ease and support the implementation process. Further details about the specific strategies the school implemented as they worked with the literacy facilitator are provided in a separate section, "Changes to Literacy Practices", later in this chapter. The emphasis placed on literacy by the principal in this school as a focus for TAI elevated the expectations for professional learning among the staff. This is another example, alongside the three schools described in Chapter 3, where the senior leaders in the school took responsibility for creating the culture among staff to implement TAI.

> *"It was important that the aspiration of continuous improvement applied to everyone as part of being a professional. Inquiry teams needed to find ways to make*

> *the risk taking of changing pedagogy and discussing the good alongside the not so good as part of the culture of professional learning. This positioned making changes as less risky."*

School culture—'what we *do* around here'—was very important in determining what teachers saw as being valued. It was important that the aspiration of continuous improvement applied to everyone as part of being a professional. Inquiry teams needed to find ways to make the risk taking of changing pedagogy and discussing the good alongside the not so good as part of the culture of professional learning. This positioned making changes as less risky. As Timperley et al. (2014, p. 20) have stated, "there is no place for blame, shame or fame". Initially, when TAI was introduced into all three schools, there was some teacher anxiety, possibly related to others knowing what they were doing, could do or were not doing. The benefits of learning from each other only started to be realised in the second year of implementation in these schools.

In the third year of implementation, groups of teachers were meeting in all of the case study schools profiled in Chapter 3. Clusters of teachers were meeting with same-subject specialists from other schools to share their resources and ideas for improving learning outcomes, including talking about specific TAI iterations and how these were modified over time.

Incremental versus large-scale change

All schools were undergoing change to varying extents. The amount and pace of change needed to be managed carefully so that teachers did not become anxious or fatigued. As Fullan (2001) has eloquently stated:

> Change is a leader's friend, but it has a split personality: its nonlinear messiness gets us into trouble. But the experience of this messiness is necessary in order to discover the hidden benefits—creative ideas and novel solutions are often generated when the status quo is disrupted. (Fullan, 2001, p. 107)

The school leaders were grappling with how to implement TAI as a process to build teacher capability and showcase changes in teaching, as evidenced by changes to student outcomes. This was not an easy task, as teachers often thought that TAI was asking them to do research (i.e. find evidence, in addition to their already busy workloads). The school leaders were also aware that for larger-scale change they needed to find ways to get more teachers involved.

The case studies illustrated in Chapter 3 pointed out some small, incremental changes that individual teachers made, as well as larger changes, particularly in professional learning, across the schools. There was some promise of more department-wide changes, spread across faculties, and wider adoption of TAI across each school as teachers became increasingly confident to share their inquiries more often. The role of the facilitators was, in part, to support the middle leaders to gain confidence in leading their teams. For example, an English facilitator's success story indicates how HODs can be key drivers and motivators for implementing TAI.

> **Success story: English facilitator**
> The HOD is leading the whole department (15 teachers) through the Teaching as Inquiry process for the first time this year. While there are a few teachers who do not acknowledge any need to change, most of the teachers within the department have shown encouraging shifts. As this is the first year of working with SSA [Secondary Student Achievement] project in English, the extent, degree and manner in which most of the teachers have engaged in TAI is encouraging. Skeptical or reluctant teachers have had to admit they are impressed by the quality of the work that has been shared by some of the other staff. Under the HOD's guidance, this critical mass of excellent practice will increase within the department.

Part of the success of TAI occurred when the question 'How do we know this made a difference?' was posed as very much part of the conversations. To help build more effective learning communities, there is scope to increase the ways facilitators mentor groups of teachers, particularly in pairs or within departments, where both resources and pedagogical successes and the achievements of students can be highlighted in tandem, creating opportunities for celebrating small successes with and alongside teachers.

Changes related to literacy

Many of the teachers indicated that TAI enabled them to consider the language of their subject and how students might use literacy tools and tasks to help them understand key concepts or key words. Sometimes the students were reluctant to read if the topic did not interest them, so one of the key roles of the facilitators was to support teachers to find out what interested the students. They suggested a range of tasks to help teachers make connections with authentic contexts.

Some facilitators interviewed reluctant learners, as illustrated by a facilitator's success story.

Success story: Science facilitator

During the interview of the focus students, they all said they were not engaged in science and most of them had not gained Achieved in their first Level 1 internal assessment on harmful microbes. They did not know what was required or how to produce a written report. They were also unable to locate suitable information for their research-based assessment.

It was agreed with the middle leader that those students who wanted to improve their grades would be given the opportunity to be reassessed using a different context. Together with the middle leader, the facilitator interviewed those students who had not passed this assessment to determine which contexts of the standard interested them. They all wanted to research microbial diseases they'd had or were of interest to them and their whānau. Booklets were provided with appropriate texts for each of these diseases. The class then deconstructed an Excellence exemplar. The students were supported to identify the links between the disease and the big biological ideas. After resitting this assessment, nearly all of the students passed [the standard] and one of the focus students gained Merit. The results were considerably better than the previous year.

After interviewing the focus students, they said that they were now more engaged in science. The students were also happier that there was more group work and a variety of teaching and learning styles used by their teacher.

There were many other examples of how teachers homed in on the language of their subject, as well as specific requirements of assessments for their subject, as indicated in the next section.

Changes to assessment practices

A specific emphasis on developing formative assessment to inform the various parts of the cycle of TAI (see Figure 1, p. 2) is worth highlighting. Many teachers from different curriculum areas chose to change the ways they looked at students' work to inform their inquiry. This means they also choose more activities to help develop the skills they had identified that students needed help with.

From a culturally responsive perspective, teachers found multiple ways to provide feedback and get feedback from their students about assessment tasks. An example of an English teacher's changes to her assessment practices, as provided by one of the English facilitators, highlights the difference this can make for students.

> **Success story: English facilitator**
> An English teacher identified a need to focus on the feedback conversation as a way of improving her students' self efficacy and achievement in writing. The realisation that feedback, as with all conversations, is a cultural construct has made her rethink her approach. In response to comments from students, she introduced more oral feedback as well as the written feedback she had given previously. This allowed students to check with her that they understood the feedback and to discuss next steps as they developed their writing and used the language of the standard and assessment criteria. Two examples of writing from one of her priority learners clearly showed a strong shift as a result of her feedback informing his understanding of success criteria. The teacher's next steps are to explore how feedback can promote independence and self-efficacy so that the students can write under exam conditions.

This story illustrates how this teacher showed a willingness to listen to her students about what would make a difference for them: oral feedback. Many teachers also provided one-to-one feedback online using Google Docs for almost immediate feedback to students, which they much appreciated. These ideas are explored further—across the enablers for priority learners, middle leaders and teachers, and for the teachers more generally in the case study schools—in a discussion on key enablers in Chapter 6.

Changes related to culturally responsive teaching

Schools and teachers usually identified classes and students who were not achieving well as their trigger for identifying what responses in teaching might help. In most cases, facilitators worked alongside the teachers to consider the achievement data, observe lessons and discuss possible strategies for improving students' outcomes. They also indicated culturally responsive approaches that were supported by key findings from the literature. A facilitator's success story with a social science head of department illustrates how they did this by focusing on reciprocity, relationship and reflection.

> **Success story: Social science facilitator (part 1)**
>
> Underachievement of Māori, Pasifika and other students was significant enough to prompt the HOD Social Sciences to act to raise student achievement as the majority of these students were performing well below the national average.
>
> The priority students were interviewed where they spoke of being disengaged—they found that some topics were boring, it wasn't clear to them about what was being taught, and no exemplars were being given to show what was expected. These students lacked motivation, self-confidence and they all had a low level of literacy skills.
>
> At the same time a group of middle leaders, including the HOD Social Sciences, formed a professional learning group within the school to support the in-depth work of raising student achievement. This group focused on culturally responsive pedagogy and what it looks like in the classroom, effective teaching and learning practices, and leadership within departments.
>
> The HOD had considered all the data, student voice and reflected on her learners and the work they were producing. This led her to inquire into effective literacy practices to support her L2 Geography class and to improve important student outcomes. As a consequence [of] discussions with the middle leader, classroom observations and

further student voice, culturally responsive pedagogy was essential to support the development of any positive outcomes. To support her in this journey, together we explored research such as the Te Kotahitanga project, Ka Hikitia, Pasifika Education Plan, Quality Teaching Research and Development reports [Ministry of Education research project for each learning area] and the BES Social Sciences research. It was through exploring these that the HOD began to see the relevance of such research and how aspects of these could be applied to her classroom practice. As a facilitator, I coached the HOD as an appropriate way to support and grow this middle leader.

The '3 Rs' of reciprocity, relationship and reflection on reality, were all going to be critical if there was going to be any significant shift in student achievement. As a high trust model developed between me and the middle leader, I was welcomed into the classroom to make observations using a tool that incorporated the Tātaiako cultural competencies. It was through these competencies that we could delve deeper into what culturally responsive pedagogy could look like.

The facilitator continued the story to indicate the success this HOD had.

Success story: Social science facilitator (part 2)

Through the readings, research and discussions, the HOD made significant progress into creating a class environment where students were collaborating, there was an enjoyment of learning, and there was a positive atmosphere with the teacher setting high expectations that were clear to the students. These students spoke of now loving their subject and how their teacher taught them was more effective. Knowing that students learn best when it is interesting and meaningful, the teacher gave students choice for many aspects of the programme— there were opportunities to choose their own contexts, as well as using placed-based contexts. Exemplars were given for assessments that gave them a very good guide as to what was expected. The teacher talked them through marking schedules. When they walked into class, a learning objective and success criteria [were] on the board and they knew clearly what was expected of them for the lesson. As the teacher began to see positive changes, she was able to target effective literacy practices to support student outcomes.

In this case, the teachers' written and verbal feedback were targeted and specific, which students found useful. Groups had been set up to provide peer assessment and effective feedback, giving students an understanding of what was expected. The teacher mentored two Māori students and one Pasifika student through the use of diary feedback to raise their achievement. The students were given a diary to use as a reflective learning tool. Once a week the teacher collected this in, looked at what the students had written and wrote a reflection back to the students in their diaries. The students felt very comfortable with this process, engaged with it and commented on the benefits of using a diary. They loved getting personalised feedback, and because it was written in a diary they couldn't lose it! The diaries enabled the teacher to build a stronger relationship with her students, and she saw them becoming more confident and positive about their progress. This led to their being more comfortable about talking in front of others, and they even began leading some of the group work.

There were also other ways that teachers embraced more culturally responsive approaches to the experiences they provided for students. Making connections with members of the community and including them as advisers and participants within the teaching programmes supported schools to develop more responsive and locally relevant content (especially School C, see Chapter 3). The need to develop more locally relevant learning experiences also provided a reason for teachers to connect positively with their local communities, and for members of their communities to feel that their opinions and knowledge counted. Bishop and Glynn (1999, pp. 198–200) stated that when working in Māori contexts:

> To develop and use a strategy that leaves people out of the conversation is to perpetuate a system that is hierarchical, that repeats the pattern of dominance and subordination that has characterised relationships in our country for too long, and that denies people legitimate representation and participation. Monocultural pedagogies developed in New Zealand on the basis of unchallenged metaphors have dominated classroom practice for much of the history of schooling in this country. (pp. 198–200)

To assist staff in connecting with and hearing from their community, the facilitator organised a meeting with other teachers who were from local iwi (tribes) to discuss the kinds of approaches and activities that would be locally relevant. The learners and principals are contributing ideas as alternatives to how teachers have taught previously and use the TAI process to identify changes in practice that can make a real difference. The facilitator wrote:

> An interest in power and voice in the English classroom has led one staff member to establish a collaborative relationship with a teacher from the local kura. The facilitator introduced the teachers during a national workshop in term two. It has become a powerful relationship enabling both teachers to learn from each other. The students from Te Kura have already shared their thoughts about how to introduce whanaungatanga [building relationships] into the classroom and this kaupapa [discussion / collective vision or philosophy] has been shared more widely in the English department. Two teachers from the English department will visit the kura to learn more from the akonga [learners] about how the competencies are outlined in Tātaiako.

Across the schools in the wider project, teachers as leaders in schools are looking for ways to be more culturally responsive. Some schools have embraced this and are progressing well, whereas others have their own internal staff cultural shifts to make in terms of the imperative to connect and listen to their communities, including how members of the community might contribute actively to learning experiences for learners.

Integrating changes with existing initiatives in a community of learning

The schools that were the subject of these case studies were all involved in multiple initiatives simultaneously. This can be problematic if teachers feel overloaded, or if they are uncertain as to which initiative they need to prioritise or whether they can integrate them simultaneously. Some of the teachers felt that when TAI was introduced, it was just another passing fad or change that they were going to be obliged to participate in, and perhaps in a couple of years there would be a new one to replace it. Some of these teachers were in change fatigue mode. So how did these principals convince people that it was useful to engage in TAI alongside other initiatives the school may have chosen to participate in?

This was a challenge for school leaders. They needed to be clear about how multiple initiatives can work synergistically. As Hipkins (2015) suggests, at the very least teachers need to be able to see how multiple initiatives for pedagogical change connect to each other. Facilitators helped at times to make these connections clearer or were able to prompt teachers to think about how their actions or learning in another initiative could be transferred to what they were planning for TAI.

Unpicking the effects or outcomes for students as a result of implementing TAI, when there were other initiatives occurring, was an evaluation dilemma for the teachers in terms of them knowing whether there was a direct cause and effect as a result of changes to their teaching. This is part of the complexity of educational research. However, the end goal was for students to participate more fully, feel confident and achieve well. The teachers report that the various ways schools developed learning communities and the ways they are beginning to connect across clusters of schools is helping them to develop further ideas for improving their teaching. They have also used these connections to share how they collected indicators of student success. In general, these included:

- improved student achievement data (informal and formal NCEA tasks)
- greater student engagement in individual tasks (and completion)
- students completing more assessment tasks than previously.

The facilitation team has reflected on the actions and progress in the first 2 years of implementation of the Secondary Student Achievement project and have considered how they can mentor and further support whole-school implementation of TAI, now in its third year. Some of the school liaison facilitators have been working more closely with the principals and deputy principals or subject specialist facilitators to support professional learning groups. The success story of one of these facilitators illustrates the mentoring and guiding role for whole-school meetings.

> **Success story: School liaison facilitator**
>
> As national director of the SSA contract I approached the principal about supporting the 'inquiry' model within established school structures and processes, and therefore build sustainability at a senior leadership level.
>
> It was suggested that the Learning Area Heads meetings would be a good place to integrate the research and practice of TAI and BES Leadership, while also supporting the establishment of Tikanga Māori practices during the meetings.
>
> Initial meetings between the facilitator and principal celebrated the 'knowledge and experience' each person could bring to this work, while also maintaining a focus on the principal's leadership goals and aspirations for the middle leaders.
>
> We agreed that I would lead and co-facilitate the first two to three meetings so that the principal could see and experience a facilitation model that gave all middle leaders a voice, managed distractions and challenged thinking and 'ways of working' in a supportive professional environment. After each meeting we met to debrief and critically evaluate the meetings.

This facilitator considered that a critical factor for the success of her work with the principal was the "professional respect" and collegiality established between them. She added that:

> Not all senior leaders are prepared to look closely at how they facilitate and lead middle leader meetings. It was a credit to the principal that she was open to this suggestion. A significant outcome has been the Principal leading discussions based on the Teaching as Inquiry framework. This has resulted in professional dialogue and decision-making processes which clearly have 'learners at the centre' and allow for assumptions to be challenged within a culture of professionalism. (Facilitator)

Summary

When teachers shared their stories with their facilitators and with each other, there was a sense that their efforts were acknowledged and valued. Collaborative inquiry was occurring mostly within departments in School A. In comparison, teachers in Schools B and C provided examples of where staff from different departments were collaboratively designing and working together on common focus areas for their priority learners.

> *"Leaders will need to be mindful, though, that when teachers collaborate, there is a greater risk of exposing teachers' practices to each other. This can have benefits and risks, which need to be managed in a positive culture of 'We can support each other to improve'."*

Collaboration and support among staff could be developed further, and have been identified in previous studies as being essential for sustainability and ongoing professional enhancement (Bishop & Berryman, 2012; Boyle, White, & Boyle, 2004; Kaser & Halbert, 2014). Leaders will need to be mindful, though, that when teachers collaborate, there is a greater risk of exposing teachers' practices to each other. This can have benefits and risks, which need to be managed in a positive culture of 'We can support each other to improve'.

The opportunities provided by this project for individual teachers to understand pedagogy more deeply—especially in terms of how changes make a difference—is starting to be realised by teachers in each of the case study schools. These opportunities are gradually aligning with departmental, faculty or school goals. The goals in the multiple layers are also being refined and have become more specific as teachers gain experience using TAI.

Guiding questions

1. Can you give a specific example of where a school leader indicated clearly why a focus on an initiative was important?
2. What might be some creative ways for teachers to share their TAI decisions and what happened?
3. How has your use of a literacy strategy changed learners' achievement?
4. Why is it important to focus on formative assessment as part of TAI? In other words, what parts of the TAI cycle does it provide information for?
5. How are you supported to develop culturally responsive approaches to teaching?
6. How could you connect with someone from the community to support the learning experiences of your students?
7. How often does your department consult members of the community about the types of experiences that might be place-based or locally relevant?

Chapter 6: Key findings

The case study schools and success stories from the wider project indicate what enabled TAI. This chapter summarises the key findings in relation to the levels and groups of participants—priority learners, teachers and middle leaders—and across schools. We deliberately used a range of methods to seek examples of how teachers' changes actively improved outcomes for priority learners. Also, in the spirit of continuous improvement, we wanted to know what the key enablers and constraints were so that we could use these to improve the support and approaches for teachers to engage with TAI.

Effectiveness was context specific and subject related, and over time there was a need to identify the specific individual needs of staff for their career development, alongside school-wide emphases. Leaders recognised that some accountability within each school for TAI was useful for indicating how TAI was valued, to provide motivation for teachers to use TAI while recognising and showcasing good examples of changes to teaching. The significance of the approach taken in this project was that teachers identified their teaching needs in relation to what their priority learners needed. As a result of small changes in their teaching, they identified specific ways in which inquiry has supported their students' learning.

The following sections outline the key enablers for the levels of participants in this initiative: priority learners, teachers and middle leaders, and communities of learners.

Key enablers for priority learners

The students interviewed in all three case study schools appreciated the fact that their teachers cared enough to want to change their teaching to help them learn more effectively. This in itself has created positive relationships between students and teachers. Some of the teachers were very surprised about how sharing their concerns with students made a positive difference to these relationships. It seems very important for students that teachers convey an ethic of care to their students about their progress.

Students had clear opinions about what they enjoyed and what they found interesting. For students in Years 9 and 10 (13–15-year-olds), the interest component of classes—both the content and how they were being asked to participate—in their opinion determined how much they learned. The students regarded the teachers' enthusiasm and interest in what they learned as a key enabler. TAI may thus provide additional focus that helps to engage teachers more with the interests of their priority learners.

Students also appreciated individual conferencing with their teachers and the ability to provide feedback to teachers about what was useful for them personally (the content and processes of learning). The conferencing worked both ways: students got to have a say, and they got to hear personal feedback about their work and next steps for learning. The benefits of these feedback loops can be incorporated into future iterations of teacher inquiry, as shown in the success story from a science teacher in School A (see Chapter 3).

There may be other ways students can provide informal feedback about what and how they are learning. They certainly appreciated being able to use Google Docs, where their teachers provided quick responses to what they had written. In many instances, students were encouraged to participate more in self-assessment, where their metacognitive awareness of their own learning was developed. Conner (2014) has shown the value of self and peer assessment for students in terms of developing their metacognitive skills, especially in relation to inquiry and essay-writing processes. Reflective tools, such as diaries, check sheets and rubrics, can be used to target the key competencies in *The New Zealand Curriculum*, such as *managing self* and *thinking*.

Some teachers used electronic resources with quiz or survey functions (e.g. Kahoot), or made use of scaffold prompts and self-feedback tools (e.g. mood boards) to help students self-assess their learning needs and development. Students liked using these tools.

The findings from this project and the literature suggest that a range of factors supported TAI, but there was no one solution or model that produced the best outcomes for students. Rather, the ideas were customised according to students' needs, and then as a result there were professional needs for their teachers.

The focus on priority learners allowed the facilitators and teachers to consider more culturally responsive pedagogies alongside aspects related to literacy, numeracy and promoting wellbeing and success. Teachers and facilitators discussed a number of changes they could make for learners by using previous research literature and thinking more deeply about how they could generate positive learning relationships with their students. As illustrated by the teacher's story in the section "Keeping Perspective" in Chapter 4, students responded when they were given clear guidance and unrelenting support. This takes some effort, which is not necessarily sustainable if applied to all students. However, when this occurred, it certainly made a huge difference to the engagement, participation and achievement of the priority learners.

Key enablers for teachers and middle leaders

The subject-specialist facilitators supported each middle leader to:

- identify the specific needs and strengths of four to five priority learners
- design specific, subject-related interventions
- identify the benefits of their changes through student participation and a range of achievement data
- share what they were doing and write success stories.

For example, a teacher commented on how the facilitator had supported him:

> I have been most impressed with the quality of the facilitator and the professional relationship that has been developed. I have been provided with a wealth of professional readings, valuable examples, teaching aids, supports and guidance. Communication has been excellent and focused upon the tasks and targets of the inquiry. (Teacher)

The self-determining and ongoing nature of improvement in teaching is gaining momentum among the whole staff in Schools B and C, and in specific departments in School A. The key drivers of this development are the commitment of the senior leaders in these schools, particularly the deputy principals, who have led and encouraged whole staff and individuals to progress with their inquiries. They have created a culture where it is safe to be focused on improving teaching, without judgement about the type or depth of reflection. The teachers in these schools have also been willing to try out inquiry—to give it a go. By identifying student success (or their own learning) from their first attempts, they have gained confidence in the process of inquiry. It has been more powerful when teacher learning was associated with student learning.

The leaders are incorporating a range of tools to consider student tracking and monitoring of achievement. They are also revising school strategic plans to include departmental strengths, challenges and shifts. Many departmental plans in these case study schools now include targets for Māori and Pasifika students, learners with special education needs, learners from low socioeconomic backgrounds, and English-language learners (ELLs). A middle leader from the schools in the wider Secondary Student Achievement project indicated how this was working for his English department:

> The department has begun what the facilitator described as the 'drill down' feature of Inquiry. [We asked] 'What are specific ethnicity features that link to performance?' There is a common belief that what is good for Māori and Pasifika students is good for all students, but there are some specific ethnicity features that are important for particular ethnicities. A Pasifika teacher in the department presented an influential video made by Pasifika students from this school on their diagnosis of learning difficulties. We heard about a preference for group work and an acknowledgment of an undue diversion of time to sport.
>
> The department, with the initial facilitator stimulus and follow-up professional discussions on ethnicity and associated 'drill down' features [using data and observations of students], has moved [us] into the richly rewarding area of inquiry as a necessary part of teaching and learning. Action research of this kind is the best means of deploying an 'assessment data for learning' strategy in the future. (Middle leader)

So the teachers as a group within this English department, considered how students differed in their needs. They used achievement data, information from observations of students' work and specific ways students said they preferred to learn (video) to help them to consider multiple modifications to their teaching. Through sharing these changes, they are providing examples to others and supporting each other with TAI.

> *"There was a sense that reflection is what good teachers do, so we might as well make it work for the students."*

As a result of participating in TAI, some of the teachers claimed that they gained enthusiasm about their work in that they gained vigour and renewed interest in their work. Students commented that they had observed this as well. There was a sense that reflection is what good teachers do, so we might as well make it work for the students. The teachers in all three schools agreed that after their second year they were only just developing the skills to seek the information they needed from students, and to align this information with their goals and changes to pedagogy. It takes time and practice to develop these skills.

While not all changes in teachers' behaviours led to immediate improvement in outcomes for students, teachers identified cognitive and affective outcomes that gave them promise and confidence to keep trying additional changes.

Key enablers for professional learning communities

> *"The role of school leaders then, is to make connections with and between stakeholders, to enrich and deepen the possibilities for how vested interests and ideas can be shared within more powerful learning communities."*

Schools, by their very nature and structure, are made up of different groups of stakeholders. Students are grouped into classes, years and subjects. Teachers are often separated or grouped—depending on how you view it— into subject areas. The existing structures of time, space and responsibilities divide the stakeholders into their parts, rather than seeing them more holistically as parts of learning communities.

The role of school leaders, then, is to make connections with and between stakeholders, to enrich and deepen the possibilities for how vested interests and ideas can be shared within more powerful learning communities (Stoll et al., 2003). Powerful, in this sense, means the ability to leverage the learning or knowledge gained among and between groups relating to the spread and speed of implementation (Wenger, McDermott & Snyder, 2002).

It is worth considering some of the assumptions and forces that Wenger (2000, p. 229) has proposed:

1. Members are bound together by their collectively developed understanding of what their community is about and they hold each other accountable to this sense of joint enterprise.
2. Members build their community through mutual engagement. They interact with one another, establishing norms and relationships of mutuality that reflect these interactions. To be competent is to be able to engage with the community and be trusted as a partner in these interactions.
3. Communities of practice have produced a shared repertoire of communal resources—language, routines, sensibilities, artefacts, tools, stories, styles, etc. To be competent is to have access to this repertoire and be able to use it appropriately.

Establishing the acceptance of communities of practice is still a challenge for the three case study schools. There are historical reasons, internal political reasons, and a desire for the status quo to remain. Teachers need to be convinced that participating in TAI and sharing this with their colleagues is worthwhile. Participating in TAI was not voluntary in these schools, but contributing to the wider professional learning community was. As Wenger et al. (2002) stated:

> Most important, communities of practice create value by connecting the personal development and professional identities of practitioners to the strategy of the organization. Successful ones deliver value to their members as well as to the organization. If it is not clear how members benefit directly from participation, the community will not thrive,

because the members will not invest themselves in it. Similarly if the community's value to the organization as a whole is not understood, it is difficult to justify resources in the community and to legitimize its voice. (p. 17–18)

The teachers, leaders and facilitators had to identify success (and we used success stories to help here) to value TAI. By considering the impact of TAI at different levels within each of the case study schools, we gained a clearer understanding of what enables progress for students, teachers and leaders as learners within a community. In these schools there were evolving cultures of a growing acceptance that TAI was part of continuous improvement for the benefit of students. However, the power of professional learning communities was only just starting to be realised at the end of the second year of implementation. The individuals were learning, but when they shared this the whole community gained. The culture that it was OK to 'shine' or provide examples was growing as part of TAI process.

In the first year there was some resistance to participating. Teachers were accustomed to being involved in professional learning, but mostly where a presenter led it. In contrast, TAI as professional learning is more aligned to what they are doing for appraisal purposes and for their requirements as a reflective practitioner for the Registered Teacher Criteria (New Zealand Teachers Council, 2010a). It was not immediately obvious to some of them that this could represent professional learning. Therefore, some convincing was needed, with the use of clear examples of TAI in practice so that teachers could see the value in participating.

The enthusiasm of the early adopters was used as a catalyst in some schools. In other schools the principal stated strongly that TAI was expected of everyone, as it was to be used as part of the school's appraisal processes. Even in schools where TAI was mandated, it took 2 years for the teachers to become skilled at developing the inquiry process. This meant that HODs had to become familiar with the process themselves before they could support others.

The sharing of teachers' learning was facilitated through paired activities, and through departmental and whole-school meetings, but only rarely in the first 2 years. In addition, the subject facilitators ran a meeting in November for teachers and heads of department for the Canterbury schools involved in the PLD. At this meeting, cultural aspects were highlighted in relation to a focus on identity, language and culture. Also, teachers had an opportunity to share their experiences, both across schools for each subject and within their school groups, and to consider wider issues such as student feedback and how student voice was informing changes to their practice. For example, a success story from a head of English described the process they undertook as a department to share their inquiries.

Success story: Head of English
The school asked our department to set up PLGs [professional learning groups] and these have been used to allow teachers to bring their inquiry findings to professional forums. We set up a problem/solution structure underpinned by the question: 'What were the problems students identified with respect to writing essays and what were potential solutions to the problems?' We had gathered student achievement information through formative tasks and then used it as a starting point for improving grades. How could we get a student from a Not Achieved grade to a secure Achieved grade? Samples of student work after hunches had been followed up were distributed to teachers. Problems identified were: inadequate planning, digression, undeveloped ideas, opacity, insufficient understanding of the function of each section of essay structure, and problems with punctuation and grammar. Remedial strategies employed were: diagrammatic planning, think/pair/share, peer support, teacher guidance, SOLO, Google Classroom (with its efficient capacity for comment), draft essays on Google Classroom used for twin purposes (i.e. proofreading as well as development of ideas in essay form).

The senior leaders in all three schools had aligned the inquiry process with their school's appraisal system. In the first year the process was somewhat forced and there was an initial resistance from some staff. In the second year all three schools took a lighter approach to goal setting, less insistence on deadlines and perhaps less accountability. The senior leaders in all three schools agreed that in the second year they were not as targeted with the requirements for appraisal, and some teachers prolonged developing their goals and focus for inquiry. On reflection, they thought the second year was too soon to hand over responsibility to the teachers, who would have benefited from some accountability measures and mentoring still being in place.

The leaders knew that it was important, as part of the accountability, to model that they were also learners. This was especially evident in School A, where the principal undertook his own inquiry and presented this to the staff as a parallel activity in the first year of TAI. The principal provided an example and established the importance of inquiry within the school. He noted that to increase engagement with TAI, the school needed multiple examples of how it worked in different subjects. He was also aware that it needed continual support from a team of staff to drive and sustain momentum to build the culture and the learning community that included the opinions of students.

Specific instances and events, when shared with colleagues, showed how these examples were important. For example, an English department (16 staff) was focusing on culturally responsive pedagogies. As part of this emphasis, students were encouraged to tell their stories about what mattered to them, to help them to convey this in their writing. An English specialist facilitator described how an HOD encouraged a Samoan/Romanian boy to write about the tension he experienced between his view of his estranged father as a violent and unfair man, and the traditional values of respect and service that are commonly seen within Samoan culture:

> The level of authenticity in the voice of this student, and the development of the idea that, as a young Samoan man, he sees no place for his father's old fashioned views in modern New Zealand—or modern Samoa— have enabled the boy to produce a very strong piece of writing. This may also form the basis of an oral presentation at some stage in the year, allowing the student to experience success in two achievement standards

Feedback from teachers indicated that they valued the opportunity to share experiences, think more deeply about aspects of their inquiries and develop further insight into the world view of Māori and Pasifika learners so that they could apply these ideas to their practice. Sharing how changes are making a difference for students is helping to sustain the project and the development of a community of learners. There is potential to enhance the way teachers and schools can learn further from each other, and with teachers in other schools, through multiple opportunities.

Building connections with parents and caregivers about their students' learning placed importance on how children's learning could be supported by the wider communities. All three schools in this study were building stronger connections with their parent and caregiver communities, creating opportunities to have open conversations about the students and their progress. There is scope to further develop working with parents so that they gain a better understanding of the approaches teachers are using and why they are using them.

If teachers take the aspirations of *The New Zealand Curriculum* seriously and advocate for learners to take more responsibility for their own learning, then the stakeholders within schools need to be clear about how they can support each other, what their reciprocal expectations are, and how members of the community will take responsibility for parts of their learning journeys.

Stoll et al. (2013) have described learning communities as a jazz ensemble. This is because, in a jazz ensemble:

> Each person's individuality is respected, each individual's talents are allowed to feature, and plenty of experimentation and improvisation takes place as the group begins to come together to create their music. Musical scores exist and guide the direction of the piece but participants are not limited to the printed page. The leader creates an environment of safety, encouragement and mutual trust that sustains the group's community spirit over time. (pp. 113–114)

Summary

The secondary schools involved with the Secondary Student Achievement project continue to operate systems and processes that are a regular part of managing a large organisation. However, TAI is helping them to make greater changes in learning outcomes at multiple levels: for priority learners, teachers and middle leaders, and across the schools.

There was no one solution for priority learners that could be applied to others, even when they seemingly had similar issues. Students had to be treated as individuals and given learning opportunities to make changes for themselves. Knowing how much guidance to give each student was a dilemma for teachers. Teachers found their own solutions, with the support of the facilitators. Some learning was transferred between pairs of teachers, those working across departments on common agendas, and within PLGs. Success using TAI as a vehicle for change depended on people at each level of influence feeling comfortable and confident enough to seek solutions that would work for them. As Harris (2002) suggested:

> Within the process of school improvement, no one can tell people what to do. They have to be allowed to search for their own solutions and to instigate and manage change inside their own institutions. (p. 18)

It was critical that, as part of the professional learning, facilitators created opportunities to work alongside senior leaders to critically inquire into the shared meaning, purpose and nature of TAI processes, especially for whole-school staff meetings and meetings for middle leaders, so that they were relevant, research-informed and supported achievement outcomes for priority learners.

Driving TAI at a whole-school level required team leadership and support for sustaining professional learning communities. The principals talked about developing the school vision as a "shared" process. They were aware of the need to connect staff to what had worked well previously, consider what actions were needed, and derive goals for projects and campaigns for specific improvements in student outcomes. As Louis and Miles (1990) have indicated, school leaders are not just problem solvers: they must also be problem seekers. Or, to put it another way, school leaders need to ask wise questions (Stoll et al., 2003).

Guiding questions

1. Can you think of an example where you made incremental change to a learning focus or to the development of a competency?
2. When might it be useful to make significant changes to approaches to teaching?
3. How does context make a difference to how you teach?
4. How are groups of teachers supported in your centre or school to develop their practice?
5. What factors need to be considered to sustain school-wide professional learning and development?

Chapter 7: Recommendations for enhancing the implementation of TAI

This chapter addresses the following questions:
1. What have we learned from this project?
    a. What were the enablers?
    b. What were the constraints?
2. Given the benefits of TAI, what are the next steps for enhancing actions so that TAI is more sustainable?
3. How can leaders support effective, ongoing professional learning?
4. How can we use TAI more effectively to address equity issues?

1. What have we learned from this project?

While there is an evolving culture of acceptance of continuous improvement for the benefit of students as part of what teachers do as professionals, there is a need to consider multiple enablers for helping teachers to undertake TAI and for all staff to take collective responsibility for students' learning. There is no doubt that teachers' development of their curiosity and enthusiasm about how their changes in teaching can improve learning have renewed their interest in teaching.

Enablers

As part of the Secondary Student Achievement project, teachers were supported to undertake mini inquiries into their teaching. They agreed that having to get evidence as part of TAI "made it more formal" but also enabled them to extend their students' needs analysis, providing impetus for them to try new things.

> *"Leaders needed to be mindful that while there were benefits from sharing TAI, there was a greater risk of exposing teachers' practices to each other. This had benefits and risks that needed to be managed in a positive culture of 'we can support each other to improve'."*

They thought collegiality had increased between inquiry partners, where two teachers were working collaboratively on an initiative or changes to teaching within their professional learning groups and at a whole-school level. Collaboration and support among staff has been identified in previous studies as being essential for sustainability and ongoing professional enhancement (Bishop & Berryman, 2012; Boyle et al., 2004; Kaser & Halbert, 2014). Leaders needed to be mindful that while there were benefits from sharing TAI, there was a greater risk of exposing teachers' practices to each other. This had benefits and risks that needed to be managed in a positive culture of "we can support each other to improve". All the teachers interviewed in these schools commented on the change in school culture that was required to make it safe to take risks in changing their teaching. They mentioned that as a result, discussing the good alongside the not so good became less risky.

> *"Taking action and responsibility for any changes to teaching enabled them to develop as more effective teachers. As their understanding of TAI grew, they gained efficacy about how they were making a difference to their learners, which built their confidence to make subsequent changes."*

Teachers were supported at multiple levels to be agents of their own professional learning. Taking action and responsibility for any changes to teaching enabled them to develop as more effective teachers. As their understanding of TAI grew, they gained efficacy about how they were making a difference to their learners, which built their confidence to make subsequent changes. The senior leaders commented on the difference between teachers who had only just begun and the increased confidence of those who had a couple of years' experience with TAI. Therefore, not only is time needed for initially conducting TAI, but there is a developmental aspect that needs to be taken into account for implementing more effective TAI. Teachers at any school will be at different stages of development and ease with using evidence for reflective practice.

Pedagogical focus for priority learners

In this project there were many different aspects of pedagogy that became the focus for teachers. Developing students' skills with respect to participation (enhancing interest), literacy and assessment capability were key emphases that supported improvement of student achievement. Because the teachers focused on priority learners, these were, by implication, students at risk of failing NCEA assessments. Therefore a focus on developing literacy skills and how to tackle assessment tasks, especially through identifying subtasks and specific skills, seemed to improve the outcomes for these students.

> *"This suggests there is more scope for teachers to help students to become more self-aware of what they are good at and what they need help with, as well as identifying next learning steps."*

It is likely that students who are already achieving well have developed strong learning-to-learn capabilities (Conner, 2014) and therefore are in less need of such targeted support. This is reinforced by other research that has demonstrated how lower-achieving students make comparatively more gains when there is a strong emphasis on learning-to-learn skills (Zohar & Ben David, 2008).

In the report of the New Zealand secondary teachers' national survey data ($n = 1,266$ teachers), Hipkins (2015) indicates that there was a weak to moderate correlation between the "growing student assessment capability" factor and how teachers guided students with talk to support their learning development. This suggests there is more scope for teachers to help students to become more self-aware of what they are good at and what they need help with, as well as identifying next learning steps. Teachers can guide students to make links between assessment demands and the learning actions students might take.

The national survey data suggested that students were not always given many opportunities to reflect on their learning or to participate in decisions about how they might learn more effectively. When students are given opportunities to develop their self-awareness, they are more likely to be conscious of what they are good at and what they need to work on as learners (Conner, 2014).

Hipkins (2015) also indicates that professional learning that challenges teachers' assumptions about the ability of weaker students is important. This is especially so to combat the assumption that weaker students might not be capable of higher-order thinking. In the schools involved in the Secondary Student Achievement project, teachers shared specific learning information about specific learners. This supported professional learning about the activities and approaches as they changed them, and teachers also learned about their students' capabilities. In some cases teachers were able to use this information about learners and apply it to learning in their own subjects.

Many teachers also found it useful to talk to students about how they learned in another subject and which bits might be useful for their subject area. In other words, the capacity for knowledge building among the teachers was doubly beneficial (both about teaching and about the students themselves).

Subject-specific support was important, especially because this related to understanding the specific requirements of subject-based assessment. In a school where the majority of students were of Pacific Island heritage, like most students they wanted more learning contexts that were of interest to them. For example, they were keen to learn more about the technology of their ancestors, so the science facilitator provided the middle leader with a Level 1 NCEA context and task based on the traditional use of levers in waka construction. Because the students had also identified that they wanted more group work, tasks were organised so that students worked in small groups to generate data.

While many of the facilitators provided literacy support, it was based on the subject matter and contexts appropriate for specific learning areas. One of the science facilitators provided a success story about this.

Success story: Science facilitator

At the start of the middle leader's inquiry, the focus students were concerned that in their previous assessments they were not learning from their failures. The students wanted more support and clarity on what was required for them to achieve and the skills needed to write a science report. Unfortunately, even after literacy support, only two students passed their practice assessment. Both these students gained Merit and had made good use of the literacy support materials.

With help from the facilitator, the middle leader worked on a strategy to address this situation. While the students who had gained Merit worked on what was required for Excellence, the remainder of the class deconstructed the language features of the two Merit exemplars from these students, making notes on key science ideas and how these were linked to data. These students then revisited their practice assessments and all of them passed. When it came to their final assessment, the pass rate and number of students gaining Merit and Excellence was much higher than the previous year. The middle leader was encouraged by the facilitator to celebrate the students' success by sending postcards home praising the students using the language of their cultural heritage.

This story was reflected many times in this project, but in relation to different subject areas. The story illustrates how praise for achieving well was offered more frequently than had been done in the past. Importantly, teachers gave different types of specific feedback on students' work as they undertook multiple assessment tasks.

In very few instances changes in teaching had immediate and obvious effects on student outcomes. However, when teachers sought evidence of changes in interest, completion of tasks, attendance in class and other changes to learning outcomes, they became more convinced that their efforts were worthwhile.

Constraints

There was a range of ways in which teachers were supported to develop their intentions—through the use of forms, student learning information from formative assessment, listening to students' responses to what interested them, and helping students to self-assess their own needs. Several teachers mentioned that filling in templates or forms for establishing TAI put them off initially. How TAI is introduced (i.e. in terms of what teachers will be required to do) can appear to some teachers to be an imposition.

Some teachers considered that the way TAI was introduced put them off at first. TAI had been promoted as a new initiative rather than what good teachers would be doing anyway. The purpose and potential gains of participating in TAI needed to be explained more clearly in the first year.

Teachers also said "We don't know what we don't know". This statement related to teachers wanting access to educational research literature. They appreciated the suggestions and recommended readings the facilitators and middle leaders provided. Often teachers needed these conversations with knowledgeable others, as has been indicated in previous studies (Levin, 2003; Timperley, 2011b). They also needed to be reminded of sources where they could find information and then share this within their PLG. Some teachers who had been involved in postgraduate courses through universities found the readings very valuable because they provided a focus and sources for key ideas to reflect on.

The initial focus on hard data to demonstrate shifts in student outcomes probably resulted from an emphasis on evidence and the promise of developing evidence-based inquiry (Timperley, 2011b). However, when teachers started to consider multiple ways to observe changes in students' learning behaviours, such as attendance information and participation in NCEA Achievement Standards, alongside achievement data, they saw changes in learning as it was evolving incrementally.

> *"...she also realised that the only person she could change was herself. This was a huge revelation, and potentially a constraint, but one that she used to help teachers learn more about what they were interested in."*

Teachers needed to experience several cycles of TAI with the support of the facilitators so that they persisted if the results were not quite as they expected. The facilitators also grew in their knowledge and understanding about their role, how to work with individual and groups of teachers and the types of guidance that was appropriate for particular student's needs. During the third year of this project, the facilitators are focusing on targeted strategies and what seems to make the most difference as they support teachers.

Many of the senior leaders in the schools involved in this project were aware of their role (as leaders) to inspire their staff and encourage them: to get ordinary people to do extraordinary things. For example, the principal in School C engaged teachers emotionally with the desired outcomes, so that teachers connected with the purpose personally. She called on previous experience in motivating people to do things for the benefit of others. However, she also realised that the only person she could change was herself. This was a huge revelation, and potentially a constraint, but one that she used to help teachers learn more about what they were interested in.

While teachers' workloads continue to be a constraining factor, the case study schools, in particular, seemed to be tempted to be involved in multiple Ministry of Education improvement projects. Where this was resisted, there was greater focus on TAI to support outcomes for priority learners. As a result, in School C, for example, the lived experiences and discoveries of the teachers in this school has renewed and rekindled the teachers' enthusiasm for teaching. The benefits overall—especially the positive outcomes for students, as indicated in the in-depth schools in Chapter 3—helped the teachers to know that their efforts brought about change.

2. Given the benefits of TAI, what are the next steps for enhancing actions so that TAI is more sustainable?

Recommendations

1. Specialist facilitators should continue to work with individual teachers and departments and enhance their communications through email and phone conversations.
2. Success stories could be developed further (by teachers in collaboration with facilitators, and teachers in pairs or groups), as a tool to share with other teachers to illustrate examples of success.
3. Timed checkpoints for staff with a mentor or senior leader regarding progress with TAI are important for supporting the teacher and for accountability.
4. Although many teachers in this study focused on identifying sub-skills and building students' self-awareness of their needs, this area of focus deserves more emphasis within TAI so that appropriate support and resources can be utilised.
5. There is scope for more teachers to connect with each other, either in pairs or in small groups, to support and enhance their inquiries. Facilitators could continue to mentor groups of teachers, particularly in pairs or within departments, to more closely align adaptations to teaching with departmental or faculty goals.
6. At a school level there could be more opportunities to share learning stories in different formats and forums, or potentially through portfolios, which could also be used to provide evidence for the New Zealand Registered Teacher Criteria.
7. Departments could find ways to disseminate information more effectively other than in face-to-face meetings so that they can use some of the department meeting time to discuss the outcomes of members' inquiries. There is also scope to share their successes in wider forums than the school (e.g. teacher associations and teacher conferences, or meetings within the TAI network).
8. There could be more collaboration between schools, particularly between subject specialists, who might have similar interests and

concerns, so that they can share what they have been trying and indicate how they know outcomes for students have improved.

9. Leaders could consider how they are supporting and further developing in terms of coherency of TAI, the capabilities and capacities of their staff, and leadership for learning at multiple levels, including students as leaders.

10. Backwards curriculum design, where teachers take more account of the principles of Universal Design for Learning (Tomlinson & McTighe, 2006), and pedagogies that support cultural connections (Macfarlane, 2004) are potential areas for further development.

3. How can leaders support effective continued professional learning?

Through participating in TAI and working with their subject facilitators, middle leaders gained experience and confidence that enabled them to lead their teams of teachers. However, they needed to experience TAI through several cycles to feel comfortable setting up and reflecting on how well their changes to teaching supported students' learning and achievement. They needed to participate in TAI themselves first, in order to gain the capabilities necessary to lead and support others to develop, implement and evaluate cycles of TAI.

In the third year of the Secondary Student Achievement project, middle leaders were using a greater range of sources of data and disaggregating the information from common tests and achievement standard results according to different learners' needs. Leaders are looking for evidence to inform their planning and programme design at a departmental level. Resulting changes in curriculum design have potentially created more opportunities for students to access learning pathways and engage in contextualised and more relevant learning experiences. There has also been greater acknowledgement of the importance of finding out about students' prior knowledge and cultural capital. The challenge lies in how senior leaders can use and leverage the positive changes occurring at a departmental level, and across faculties, to inform shifts within the school and across clusters of schools.

The aspects relating to the next steps that leaders could consider in this project can also be informed by the ERO report on the evaluation of TAI in 82 primary schools, 26 secondary schools and five composite schools (ERO, 2012). The summary report indicated that next steps for school leaders should be to:

1. review, periodically, the extent to which teaching as inquiry is being used in the school, with the purpose of identifying inquiry practices that are positively impacting on students' learning, and aspects of practice that could be improved
2. extend teachers' understanding of inquiry approaches and the ways these can be used to improve learning and teaching, particularly for students whose learning should be accelerated
3. establish expectations and guidelines for planning and evaluation that have a clear focus on using analysed assessment information to bring about improved learning outcomes for students
4. access support to further develop teachers' understanding of *The New Zealand Curriculum*. (p.2)

As a result of the recommendations in this ERO report, the Secondary Student Achievement project funded support for teachers to undertake TAI with subject-specific advice and guidance from the facilitation team. Hipkins (2015) points out that teachers need deep subject expertise if they are to develop students' capacities to reflect on their own strengths and identify what they need help with. Support that is subject specific takes account of disciplinary aims and contextual factors. Therefore this model is likely to be beneficial for targeted professional learning in secondary settings in the future.

Previous studies and examples of TAI have also indicated that teachers need multiple cycles of experience to feel comfortable with the TAI process (Halbert & Kaser, 2013; Timperley, 2011b). In this project, middle leaders also needed ongoing 'seeding' of ideas from the facilitators to identify aspects that could be considered across small groups of teachers, departments or faculties.

> *"Each teacher's focus on four to five priority learners in one class, as mentioned previously, made TAI manageable. Previously the teachers considered they had not directly monitored the effects their*

> *changes in teaching had on individual students. This shift in focus has proved very useful in terms of both targeting students' specific needs and in redesigning and implementing strategies to support learning development."*

Each teacher's focus on four to five priority learners in one class, as mentioned previously, made TAI manageable. Previously the teachers considered they had not directly monitored the effects their changes in teaching had on individual students. This shift in focus has proved very useful in terms of both targeting students' specific needs and in redesigning and implementing strategies to support learning development. So while there was very much a focus on individual students, leaders also needed to consider the extent to which the needs of students were similar across different classes and what could be shared and learned in terms of both specific interventions and teacher learning at a small group level.

Although teachers did not explicitly use the framework from the findings of the cross-country case studies on innovative learning environments (OECD, 2013), they were using many of these principles in practice. These seven principles of learning were derived from multiple international studies on cognition, emotion and learning sciences in schooling systems around the world. They could be used as a framework of reference and understanding for TAI. They are:

1. learners at the centre
2. the social nature of learning
3. emotions matter in learning—(especially motivation and engagement)
4. individual differences must be recognised
5. every learner needs to be stretched without being overloaded
6. assessment for learning is essential
7. building horizontal connections creates meaning.

These principles are certainly reflected in *The New Zealand Curriculum*. They could be used for future iterations of the Secondary

Student Achievement project, just as Kaser and Halbert (2014) have indicated for their TAI project in Canada. We would also want to add a dimension or principle related to developing localised curriculum that reflects the aspirations and backgrounds of members of the local community.

4. How can we use TAI more effectively to address equity issues?

In New Zealand there is a moral imperative to raise the achievement of those who are not achieving well, for whatever reason. As part of this agenda it is very important to connect with the worlds (communities/cultures) to which students belong. This is consistent with the principles promoted through kaupapa Māori theories and pedagogies (Bishop & Berryman, 2006) and the Pasifika education priorities of belonging to a learning community (Fletcher, Parkhill, Fa'afoi & Taleni, 2008). It also aligns the idea of making horizontal connectedness more explicit in learning situations, as emphasised in the OECD cross-country case studies on innovative learning environments (OECD, 2013).

Listening to members of the community about what is important to them can enable continued stakeholder engagement with education, which may extend learning experiences beyond those traditionally thought to be important. We must acknowledge the importance of different backgrounds, talents, cultures and beliefs, respect diversity and different solutions, build on people's strengths, and promote whanaungatanga (collegial support), fono, family and community as integral to educational success.

Conclusion

By considering the impact of TAI we have gained a clearer understanding, through specific success stories, of what enabled progress for teachers and students in these schools. It took time and persistence, coaching, sharing—and some risk taking. The teachers in all three case study schools agreed that after their second year they were only just developing the skills to seek the information they needed about their priority learners and to align this information with their goals and changes to pedagogy. They agreed it takes time and practice to develop these skills.

Some of the teachers were more enthusiastic and had gained vigour and renewed interest in their work as a result of their inquiries. Students commented that they had observed this change in their teachers as well. As a result, teachers said they have become more curious about students in their other classes, and they want to find out more information about them to inform their planning and support of student learning.

While there is an evolving culture of acceptance of continuous improvement for the benefit of students as part of what teachers do as professionals, there is a need to consider how the multiple enablers can help teachers to undertake TAI more directly. There is an even stronger moral imperative to work closely with those priority learners who, without the attention and support of caring teachers, might slip out of the system.

The effectiveness of teachers' professional learning was enhanced when they identified the needs of their priority learners quite specifically, were supported to design specific subject-related interventions, saw the benefits of their changes through student participation and achievement data, shared what they were doing, and were supported at a whole-school level. These findings are consistent with previous studies about teachers enacting inquiry in their teaching (Carnell & Lodge, 2002; Conner & Duncan, 2013). We are very fortunate that the New Zealand education system enables teachers to be leaders of their own learning, because this gives them the freedom and flexibility to design their own localised and personalised curriculum for their learners. This is very rare throughout the world, and as a nation we should celebrate this more and utilise it for the benefit of the students.

References

Bailey, M. (2014). *Time to learn.* The Hechinger Report. Retrieved from http://hetchingerreport.or/special-reports/time-to-learn/

Bandura, A. (1997). *Self-efficacy: The exercise of control.* New York, NY: W. H. Freeman Publishers.

Bishop, R., & Berryman, M. (2006). *Culture speaks: Cultural relationships and classroom learning.* Wellington: Huia.

Bishop, R., & Berryman, M. (2012). *Te Kotahitanga: Investigating the sustainability of the Te Kotahitanga Professional Development Project.* Auckland: National Institute for Research Excellence in Māori Development and Advancement, University of Auckland.

Bishop, R., & Glynn, T. (1999). *Culture counts: Changing power relations in education.* Palmerston North: Dunmore Press.

Blankstein, A. M., & Noguera, P. (2015). Achieving excellence through equity for every student. In A. M. Blankstein and P. Noguera (Eds.), *Excellence through equity: Five principles of courageous leadership to guide achievement for every student,* (pp. 3–30). Thousand Oaks, CA: Corwin/Sage.

Boyle, B., White, D., & Boyle, T. (2004). A longitudinal study of teacher change: What makes professional development effective? *Curriculum Journal, 15*(1), 45–68.

Bransford, J. D., Brown, A. L., & Cocking, R.R. (1999). *How people learn: brain, mind, experience and school.* Washington, D.C.: National Academy Press. http://www.nap.edu/open book/0309065577/html/index.html

Carnell, E., & Lodge, C. (2002). *Supporting effective learning.* London, UK: Sage.

Clandinin, D. J., & Connelly, F. M. (2000). *Narrative inquiry.* San Francisco, CA: Jossey Bass.

Conner, L. N. (2013). Meeting the needs of diverse learners in New Zealand. *Preventing School Failure, 57*(3), 157–161.

Conner, L. N. (2014). Students' use of evaluative constructivism: Comparative degrees of intentional learning. *International Journal of Qualitative Studies in Education, 27*(4), 472–489. Retrieved from http://dx.doi.org/10.1080/09518 398.2013.771228.

Conner, L., & Duncan, J. (2013). Introduction. In J. Duncan & L. Conner (Eds.), *Research partnerships in early childhood education: Teachers and researchers in collaboration* (pp. 1–10). New York, NY: Palgrave Macmillan.

Covey, S. M. R. (2006). *The speed of trust.* New York, NY: Free Press.

Cowie, B., Hipkins, R., Keown, P., & Boyd, S. (2011). *The shape of curriculum change: A short discussion of key findings from the Curriculum Implementation Studies (CIES) project.* Unpublished report for the Ministry of Education.

Darling-Hammond, L., Wei, R. C., Andree, A., Richardson, N., & Orphanos, S. (2009). *Professional learning in the learning profession: A status report on teacher development in the United states and abroad.* Stanford, CA: National Staff Development Council and the School Redesign Network at Stanford University.

Day, C. (1999). *Developing teachers: The challenges of life-long learning.* London, UK: Falmer Press.

Desimone, L. M. (2009). Improving impact studies of teachers' professional development: Toward better conceptualizations and measures. *Educational Researcher, 38*(3), 181–199. doi: 10.3102/0013189X08331140

ERO. (2010). *Directions for learning: The New Zealand curriculum principles and teaching as inquiry.* Wellington: Author.

ERO (2012). *Teaching as inquiry: Responding to learners.* Wellington: Author.

ERO (2014). *Towards equitable outcomes in secondary schools: good practice.* ERO Report May, 2014. Wellington: Author.

Fletcher, J., Parkhill, F., & Fa'afoi, A. (2005). What factors promote and support Pasifika children in their reading and writing? *set: Research Information for Teachers, 2,* 2–8.

Fletcher, J. F., Parkhill, F. F., Fa'afoi & Taleni, L. T. (2008). Influences on Pasifika students' achievement in literacy. *set: Research Information for Teachers, 1,* 4–9.

Fullan, M. (2001). *Leading in a culture of change.* San Francisco, CA: Jossey-Bass.

Fullan, M. (2007). *The new meaning of educational change.* (4th ed.). New York, NY: Teachers College Press.

Fullan, M., & Hargreaves, A. (2012). *Professional capital: Transforming teaching in every school.* New York, NY: Teachers College Press.

Halbert, J., & Kaser, L. (2012). *Inquiring learning environments: New mindsets required.* Retrieved from http://youngreaders.ca/downloads/CSE%20Seminar%20Paper%20214_U-1.pdf

Halbert, J., & Kaser, L. (2013). *Spirals of inquiry: For equity and quality.* Vancouver, British Columbia: BCPVPA. Retrieved from http://www.bcpvpa.bc.ca/node/108

Haque, B. (2014). *Changing our secondary schools.* Wellington: NZCER Press.

Hargreaves, A. (1994). *Changing teachers: Changing times.* London, UK: Cassell.

Hargreaves, A. (2015). The iniquity of inequity. In In A. M. Blankstein & P. Noguera (Eds.), *Excellence through equity: Five principles of courageous leadership to guide achievement for every student* (pp. 273–288). Thousand Oaks, CA: Corwin/Sage.

Harris, A. (2002). *School improvement: What's in it for schools?.* London, UK: RoutledgeFalmer.

Hipkins, R. (2015). *Learning to learn in secondary classrooms.* Wellington: New Zealand Council for Educational Research.

Kaser, L., & Halbert, J. (2014). Creating and sustaining inquiry spaces for teacher learning and system transformation. *European Journal of Education, 49*(2), 206–217.

Levin, B. (2003). *Case studies of teacher development: An in-depth look at how thinking about pedagogy develops over time.* Mahwah, NJ: Lawrence Erlbaum Associates.

Levin, B. (2010). How to change 5,000 schools. In A. Hargreaves, A. Liberman, M. Fullan, & D. Hopkins (Eds.), *Second international handbook of educational change* (pp. 309–322). London, UK: Springer.

Loucks-Horsley, S., Stiles, K. E., Mundry, S., Love, N., & Hewson, P. (2010). *Designing professional development for teachers of science and mathematics* (3rd Ed.). Thousand Oaks, CA: Corwin/Sage.

Louis, K. S., & Miles, M.B. (1990). *Improving the urban high school: What works and why.* New York, NY: Teachers College Press.

Macfarlane, A. (2004). *Kia hiwa rā!: Listen to culture: Māori students' plea to educators.* Wellington: NZCER Press.

Ministry of Education. (2007). *The New Zealand curriculum for English-medium teaching and learning in years 1–13.* Wellington: Learning Media.

Ministry of Education. (2012a). *Ka hikitia—Accelerating success 2013–2017: The Māori education strategy.* Wellington: Author.

Ministry of Education. (2012b). *Pasifika education plan 2013–2017.* Wellington: Author.

Ministry of Education. (2012c). *The case for system-wide improvement for all learners, teachers and leaders.* Wellington: Author.

Muijs, D., Day, C., Harris, A., & Lindsay, G. (2004). Evaluating CPD: An overview. In C. Day & J. Sachs (Eds.), *International handbook on the continuing professional development of teachers* (pp. 291–310). Maidenhead, UK: Open University Press.

New Zealand Teachers Council. (2010a). *New Zealand Registered Teacher Criteria*. Wellington: Author. Retrieved from http://www.teacherscouncil.govt.nz/content/graduating-teacher-standards-english-rtf-38kb

New Zealand Teachers Council. (2010b). *Tātaiako—Cultural competencies for teachers of Māori learners: A resource for use with the Graduating Teacher Standards and Registered Teacher Criteria*. Retrieved from http://www.teacherscouncil.govt.nz/content/t%C4%81taiako-cultural-competencies-teachers-m%C4%81ori-learners-resource-use-graduating-teacher

OECD. (2013). *Innovative learning environments, educational research and innovation*. Paris, France: OECD Publishing.

Robinson, V., Hohepa, M., & Lloyd, C. (2009). *School leadership and student outcomes: Identifying what works and why*. Wellington: Ministry of Education.

Rozenszajn, R., & Yarden, A. (2014). Expansion of biology teachers' pedagogical content knowledge (PCK) during a long-term professional development program. *Research in Science Education, 44*(1), 189–213. doi: 10.1007/s11165-013-9378-6

Shields, C. M., Bishop, R., & Mazawi, A. E. (2005). *Pathologizing practices: The impact of deficit thinking on education*. New York, NY: P. Lang.

Stoll, L., Fink, D., & Earl, L. (2003). *It's about learning (and it's about time): What's in it for schools?* London, UK: RoutledgeFalmer.

Timperley, H. (2011a). Knowledge and the leadership of learning. *Leadership and Policy in Schools, 10*(2), 145–170. doi: 10.1080/15700763.2011.557519

Timperley, H. (2011b). *Realizing the power of professional learning*. Maidenhead, UK: Open University Press.

Timperley, H., Kaser, L., & Halbert, J. (2014). *A framework for transforming learning in schols: Innovation and the spiral of inquiry*. Melbourne, VIC: Centre for Strategic Education.

Timperley, H., Wilson, A., Barrar, H., & Fung, I. (2007). *Teacher professional learning and development: Best evidence synthesis iteration*. Wellington: Ministry of Education.

Tomlinson, C, A., & McTighe, J. (2006). *Integrating differentiated instruction and undrstanding by design.* Alexandria, USA: Association for Supervision and Curriculum Development.

Turvey, K. (2013). *Narrative ecologies: Teachers as pedagogical tool makers.* London, UK, & New York, NY: Routledge.

Wenger, E. (2000). Communities of practice and social learning systems. *Organization, 7*(2), 225–246.

Wenger, E., McDermott, R., & Snyder, W. (2002). *Cultivating communities of practice: A guide to managing knowledge.* Boston, MA: Harvard Business School Press.

Zohar, A., & Ben David, A. (2008). Explicit teaching of meta-strategic knowledge in authentic classroom contexts. *Metacognition Learning, 3,* 59–82.

Biographical information

Professor Lindsey Conner is the Director of the Science and Technology Education Research hub at the University of Canterbury. She has wide interests in educational reform and educational leadership and is supporting the EDPlus (University of Canterbury) and Te Tapuae o Rehua consortium, alongside colleagues at the University of Otago, to showcase examples of where TAI was working in secondary schools.

Index

A

accountability
  of school leaders 13
  of teachers 58, 59, 75, 105, , 113, 123
achievement enablers 36
  case study School A 46–47
  case study School B 59–61
  case study School C 72–73
achievement of students
  see also New Zealand National Certificate of Educational Achievement (NCEA); priority learners: outcomes of teaching changes; Secondary Student Achievement project; success stories
  in case study schools 33, 42–43, 47, 49, 51–52, 56–57, 67–69, 72–73, 78, 107
  and culturally responsive teaching 97–100
  geography class 5,72-73, 97
  health class 22, 23, 24
  history class 88
  Māori students 22, 23, 24, 42, 43, 57, 59, 66, 67, 68–69, 88, 99
  praise from teachers 55, 120
  science classes 24–25, 39, 95, 120
  social science classes 40
  and socioeconomic status 10
  use of achievement information 25, 36, 47, 64–65, 71, 76, 87, 89, 107, 109, 112, 121, 124, 125, 128
agency
  students 55 (*see also* student voice)
  teachers 7, 22, 56, 70, 117
appraisal
  decoupled from professional learning 14
  link with TAI 37, 51, 57, 58, 59, 63, 65, 66, 79, 112–13
  peer appraisal 62
  student outcomes 37
assessment 70, 77, 81, 101
see also achievement of students; New Zealand National Certificate of Educational Achievement (NCEA)
  capability 118–19, 120
  changes to practices 89, 96–97
  criteria 26, 47, 54, 80, 89, 98
  data 36, 47, 64–65, 71, 76, 89, 107, 108, 109, 112, 121, 124, 125, 128
  formative 3, 23, 24, 39, 47, 52, 55, 60, 81, 89, 96, 112, 121
  in history 87-88
  in PE 40–41
  in mathematics 41
  in science 39
  in social science 40
  New Zealand Curriculum section on assessment 89
  peer assessment 106
  reassessment 47, 95
  self-assessment 106, 107, 121
  student involvement 11
  summative 23, 25, 39, 52, 60, 61
asTTle tests 73, 76
AVAILLL reading programme 73

B

barriers to TAI implementation 48–49, 61–62, 75–77

Index

Building on Success interventions 22, 63

C

caring, by teachers 25, 30, 44, 45, 47, 50, 61, 72, 106, 128
The Case for System-wide Improvement (Ministry of Education) 10, 12, 27, 131
case study schools
    characteristics 32–34, 36, 49, 62
    collaboration and support among staff 75, 84, 102–03, 117, 123, 130
    constraints viii, 105, 116, 121–22
    enablers vi, 24, 34–36, 43-47, 57-59, 69, 77, 84, 127–28
    key enablers for priority learners 106–07
    key enablers for professional learning communities 109–14
    key enablers for teachers and middle leaders 107–09
    pedagogical focus for priority learners 118–20, 127
    summary 77–79
case study schools: School A 36
    barriers to TAI implementation 48–49, 105, 116, 121-122
    description 36–37
    enablers 42–48, 113, 116–18
    focus for inquiry 37–41
    school leadership 37
case study schools: School B 49
    barriers to TAI implementation 61–62
    description 50
    enablers 56–61, 83–84
    focus for inquiry 53–55
    school leadership 51–53, 55, 57–58, 59, 61–62, 86
case study schools: School C
    barriers to TAI implementation 75–77
    description 62–63
    enablers 67–75
    focus for inquiry 65–66
    school leadership 63–65, 74, 122
coaching, reflective 49
collaboration
    see also communities of learners; professional learning groups (PLGs)
    between student, teacher and organisation in TAI 8, 17
    between teachers 11, 26–28, 37, 60, 65, 69, 74–75, 79, 82, 87, 93, 94, 100, 102–03, 113–14, 117, 123
    between teachers and facilitators 70, 71, 83–84, 93, 123
communities of learners x, 13, 28, 111, 127
    see also professional learning and development; professional learning groups (PLGs)
    in case study schools 41–42, 55–56, 66–67, 78, 102–03
    changes related to cultural responsiveness 97–100
    changes related to literacy 95–96
    incremental *versus* large-scale change 93–94
    integrating changes with existing initiatives 100–02
    key enablers for professional

learning communities 109–14
supporting the team 91–93
community connections and
   liaison 32, 44–45, 50, 63, 67, 69,
   99–100, 114, 127
context
   authentic 95, 113, 119
   basis for teacher actions 6–7
   context-relevant advice 4
   individual school contexts 18, 33,
   84
contextual enablers 36
   case study School A 47–48
   case study School B 61
   case study School C 74–75
critical reflection 2, 5, 15, 28
   see also reflection; and entries
   beginning reflective ...
critical thinking 41
cultural competence and
   responsiveness 9–10, 16, 59, 81,
   96, 97–100, 107, 112, 113
culture of schools and teaching 8, 14,
   17, 28, 30, 50–51, 55, 57–58, 69,
   74, 92–93, 108, 117
curriculum design 3, 11, 16, 49, 65,
   107, 124, 128
curriculum implementation 85

D
deciles 62
decision making 3, 12, 32, 64, 102
developmental enablers 35
   case study School A 45–46
   case study School B 58–59
   case study School C 69–72
diaries 99, 106
digital dashboards 72

E
Education Review Office (ERO) 2,
   34–35, 36, 67
   evaluation of school leadership 13–
   14
   evaluation of TAI 3, 19, 124–25
e-learning 67, 71–72, 75
enablers 34–36, 77, 84, 116–18
   case study School A 42–48, 49
   case study School B 56–61, 83–84
   case study School C 67–75
   key enablers for priority
      learners 106–07
   key enablers for professional
      learning communities 109–14
   key enablers for teachers and middle
      leaders 107–09
engagement of students 10, 30, 77, 80,
   101, 107, 120, 126
   see also interest component of classes
   case study School A 36, 38–39, 41,
   42, 45, 46, 49
   case study School B 60
   case study School C 63, 65, 71,
   72, 76
   health classes 23
   mathematics 41
   science 24–25, 38–39, 60, 73, 95
   social science 97–99
English facilitators' success stories 94,
   96
English HOD success story 112
English Language Learners (ELLs) 39,
   53, 66, 68, 72–73, 77, 81, 108
equity 1, 7, 9, 10, 57, 127
evaluation 6–7, 13, 30
   see also Education Review Office
   (ERO)
   evidence-based 4, 8, 12, 22, 25,

29, 36, 37, 47, 54, 64–65, 71, 76, 82–83, 87, 89, 94, 101, 107, 109, 112, 116–17, 120, 121
    feedback loops 8, 17, 19, 28–29
    of school leadership 13–14
    of TAI 3, 8, 19, 28–29
external drivers 35
    case study School A 42–43
    case study School B 56–57
    case study School C 67–68

F
facilitators 33–34, 58, 62, 101
    see also subject facilitators (advisers)
    school liaison facilitator success story 102
fading guidance approach 49, 83–84
families *see* parents and whānau/families
feedback
    diaries 99, 106
    loops 8, 17, 19, 28–29, 85, 86, 87, 106
    to students 26, 39, 47, 51, 52, 59, 60, 61, 72, 74, 81, 85, 96–97, 99, 106, 112, 120
    to teachers 26, 36, 46, 54, 61, 74, 79, 85, 96, 106
formative assessment 3, 23, 24, 39, 47, 52, 55, 60, 81, 89, 96, 112, 121

G
goal setting, students 56
Google Classroom 112
Google Docs 26, 52, 67, 74, 81, 82, 96–97, 106

H
health learning area 52, 65

teacher's success story 22–24
Hechinger Report 11
history teacher success story 87–88

I
ICT 16, 63, 78
industry qualifications 71
inequity *see* equity
innovative learning environments project (OECD) 126–27
inquiry mindset 1–2
interest component of classes 25–26, 41, 49, 70, 72, 81, 87, 95, 98, 106, 118, 120
    see also engagement of students

K
Ka Hikitia—Accelerating Success 2013–2017 (Ministry of Education) 9, 98

L
leadership *see* school leadership
learning-to-learn capabilities 118
literacy 20, 77, 80, 82, 90, 118
    changes related to 95–96, 107
    facilitator success stories 14–15, 86, 92
    girls 55, 60
    health contexts 22–23
    mathematics 41
    PE 40–41
    science 38, 39, 44, 48–49, 60, 95, 120
    social science 40
    teaching resources 23, 41, 44, 47, 52, 54, 60, 67, 95
    whole-school emphasis 91–92

M

Māori
- in case study schools 32, 42, 43, 50, 51, 53, 57, 62, 63, 66, 77, 88, 108, 113
- community involvement 99–100
- culture 32, 37, 51, 59, 63
- kaupapa Māori theories and pedagogy 127
- priority learners 15, 22–24, 32, 39, 42, 53, 66, 88, 108, 113
- student achievement 22, 23, 24, 42, 43, 57, 59, 66, 67, 68–69, 88, 99
- student retention rates 10
- success as Māori 36, 37
- young people 10

mathematics 38, 41, 65
Mau ki te ako project 15–16
middle leaders 4–5, 15, 16, 94, 95, 97–99, 102, 115, 120, 124
- in case study schools 42, 52–53, 54, 58, 83, 86
- key enablers 107–09

Ministry of Education 3, 15, 22, 34, 69, 122
- Building on Success interventions 22, 63
- *The Case for System-wide Improvement* 10
- *Ka Hikitia—Accelerating Success 2013–2017* 9, 98
- *Pasifika Education Plan* 9, 98
- Quality Teaching Research and Development reports 98

moral imperative 8, 12

N

narratives, as support for inquiry 26–28, 34, 46
see also success stories

New Zealand Curriculum 2, 19, 78, 89, 106–07, 114, 125, 126
- Mau ki te ako project 15
- support of diversity 9

New Zealand National Certificate of Educational Achievement (NCEA) 10, 20, 22–23, 26, 33
- case study School A 42–43
- case study School B 52, 55, 56–57, 59–60
- case study School C 63, 66, 68–69, 71, 73
- external drivers for achievement 35, 42–43, 68–69
- preparation for internal assessment 44
- risk of failure 118
- science 24–25, 39, 119

New Zealand Qualifications Authority (NZQA) 35
Scholarships 36, 73

New Zealand Teachers Council
- accreditation requirements 35
- cultural competencies 10
- Registered Teacher Criteria 57, 111, 123
- *Tātaiako* 9, 98, 100

Ngai Tahu 15

O

observation
- of students 4, 109
- of teachers 54–55, 61, 62, 97, 98

OECD innovative learning environments project 126–27

P

parents and whānau/families, communicating with 17, 32, 37, 40, 44–45, 50–51, 114, 127

Pasifika Education Plan (Ministry of Education) 9, 98

Pasifika priority learners 15, 81, 99, 113, 119, 127
  in case study schools 39, 42, 43, 50, 53, 62, 66, 68–69, 77, 108

pedagogical changes 2, 7, 16, 24–26, 28, 37, 54, 62, 64–65, 89–90, 91, 103, 107, 127–18
  see also priority learners: outcomes of teaching changes; subject facilitators (advisers)
  assessment practices 89, 96–97
  based on student needs 28–29, 30, 49, 65, 66–67, 71, 73, 77–78, 80, 82–83, 86–89, 107, 109, 117, 126
  culturally responsive teaching 97–100
  and focus for inquiry 86–89, 118–20, 128
  incremental *versus* large-scale 93–94
  integrating changes with existing initiatives 100–02
  outcomes rarely immediate and obvious 91, 120
  and school culture 92–93
  spirals of change 16, 29
  and teacher efficacy and confidence 7, 117–18, 127–28
  willingness and flexibility of teachers 84–85

physical education (PE) 38, 40–41, 52, 73

place-based contexts 72

principals 12–15, 37, 51, 63–65, 67, 74, 92, 101, 102, 111, 113, 115, 122

priority learners
  see also student needs
  case study School A 37–48
  case study School B 49, 50, 51, 52, 53–55, 57, 59–60, 61–62
  case study School C 63, 64–68
  changes in teachers' beliefs 48–49, 80, 81, 119
  focus on small number of learners 2, 11–12, 21–24, 30, 42, 65, 87–89, 107, 126
  importance of addressing needs 9–12, 20, 24–26, 77
  key enablers 106–07
  Mau ki te ako project 15–16
  outcomes of teacher collaboration 11, 26–28, 37, 74–75
  outcomes of teacher professional development 6–7, 8, 11, 16–17, 27, 33, 34, 38, 41–42, 69–72, 74, 79, 112, 115
  TAI process for 2–4, 12, 20, 127–28

priority learners: outcomes of teaching changes 6–7, 8, 28–29, 30, 47, 49, 52, 73, 77–78, 79, 109
  see also achievement of students; evaluation; success stories
  assessment practices 96–97
  cultural responsiveness 97–100, 107
  and focus for inquiry 37–41, 53–55, 65–66, 87–89, 118–20
  incremental *versus* large-scale change 93–94

individual solutions 114–15
integrating changes with existing initiatives 101–02
literacy 95–96
outcomes rarely immediate and obvious 91, 120
and teacher efficacy and confidence 109, 117–18, 122
willingness and flexibility of teachers 84–85
procedural enablers 35
  case study School A 44–45
  case study School B 57–58
  case study School C 69
process-writing skills 20–21
professional learning and development
  see also communities of learners; enablers; Secondary Student Achievement project; subject facilitators (advisers); teaching as inquiry (TAI)
  benefits 8, 16–17
  continuous 28, 54, 79, 92–93, 111
  designing 3
  iterative, discursive and reflective components 85
  school leadership involvement 13, 14, 17, 92
  teacher choice of area 7
  whole-school emphases 91–92
professional learning communities see communities of learners
professional learning groups (PLGs) 22, 87, 97, 101, 112, 115
  case study School B 54, 55, 57–58, 60
  case study School C 66–67, 69, 70, 71–72, 74–75
  use of research 121

Q

Quality Teaching Research and Development reports 98

R

reading 55, 73
  authentic contexts 95
  challenges for English Language Learners 81
  success story 82
reflection 54, 97, 98
  critical 2, 5, 15, 28
  teams 91
reflective coaching 49
reflective learning 56, 99, 106–07, 119
reflective practice 58, 76, 79, 86, 109
Registered Teacher Criteria 57, 111, 123
research, use in designing programmes and interventions 3, 21, 77, 97, 98, 107, 115, 121
resource development and use 5, 17, 44, 47
  digital resources 40–41, 107
  literacy 23, 41, 44, 47, 52, 54, 60, 67, 95
  science 48
retention rates 10
risks
  school leadership 84, 117
  teachers 14, 29, 84, 93, 103, 117, 127
risk-taking 22,,117, 127

S

scaffolding 5, 52, 107
Scholarships (NZQA) 36, 73
school leadership
  see also middle leaders; principals;

senior leaders
   case study School A 36, 37
   case study School B 51–53, 55, 57–58, 59, 61–62, 83–84, 86
   case study School C 63–65, 67, 70, 74, 122
   and culture of professional learning 17, 78
   importance 12–15
   integrating changes with existing initiatives 100–02
   and risks of TAI 84, 117
   role relating to school stakeholders 110
   support of, and involvement in, TAI 32–33, 78, 79, 86, 91, 92, 94, 101–02, 108, 111, 112–13, 115, 122, 124–27

schools
   see also case study schools
   collaboration between 46, 123–24
   culture 8, 14, 17, 28, 30, 50–51, 55, 57–58, 69, 74, 92–93, 108, 117
   retention rates 10
   school-wide TAI implementation 4
   stakeholder groups 8, 17, 109–10, 114, 127
   structures 8, 14, 56, 102, 109–10

science
   authentic context 119
   facilitator success stories 95, 120
   literacy 38, 39, 44, 48–49, 60, 95, 120
   student engagement 24–25, 38–39, 60, 73, 95
   student goal setting 56
   teacher's reflection 46
   teacher's success stories 24–25, 45

Secondary Student Achievement project 3, 4, 12, 15–18, 32, 49, 63, 78, 92, 94, 101, 108, 114, 116, 119, 124, 125, 126–27

senior leaders 12, 17, 108, 112–13, 115, 122, 123, 124
   in case study schools 33, 34, 42, 51–52, 54, 55, 57–58, 59, 61–62, 64, 65, 78, 79

simplexity 6
social science 38, 40, 65, 74
   facilitator success stories 72–73, 97–99
socioeconomic status 10, 15, 77, 108
special education needs (SEN) 15, 37, 39, 53, 66, 77, 108
spirals of change 16, 29
stakeholder groups, schools 8, 17, 109–10, 114, 127
structural enablers 35
   case study School A 44–45
   case study School B 57–58
   case study School C 69
student engagement *see* engagement of students
student needs
   as basis for TAI 6–8, 16, 17, 30, 105
   general needs of larger student groups 91–92
   identifying 3, 4, 9, 19–21, 24, 30, 49, 52, 65, 80, 81, 87, 123, 124, 128
   identifying through "chats in the playground" 72
   importance of addressing 9–12, 20, 24–26, 49, 80
   multiple needs 87
   teaching changes based on 28–29,

30, 49, 65, 66–67, 71, 73, 77–78, 80, 82–83, 86–89, 107, 109, 117, 126
student voice 22, 26, 53, 54, 56, 65, 79, 97, 98, 112, 113, 121
subject facilitators (advisers) 3, 4–6, 7, 15–18, 34, 111–12, 119–20, 122, 123, 125
- case study School A 37–38, 41, 44, 45, 46–47
- case study School B 53, 55, 58, 60, 62, 83–84
- case study School C 65, 69, 71, 72–73, 75, 76
- collaboration between 123–24
- English facilitator success stories 94, 96
- health teacher success story 22–23, 24
- importance to success of TAI 77
- literacy facilitator success stories 14–15, 86, 92
- middle leader support 107–09, 120
- reading success story 82
- resource development 47
- roles 80–84, 94, 97, 101
- science facilitator success stories 95, 120
- social science facilitator success stories 72–73, 97–99
success stories 5–6, 26–28, 32, 34, 111, 123, 127
- English facilitators 94, 96
- Head of English 112
- health teacher 22–24
- history teacher 87–88
- literacy facilitators 14–15, 86, 92
- reading facilitator 82
- school liaison facilitator 102

science facilitators 95, 120
science teachers 24–25, 45
social science facilitators 72–73, 97–99
teacher in second year of TAI 45
summative assessment 23, 25, 39, 52, 60, 61

T

Tātaiako (New Zealand Teachers Council) 9, 98, 100
Te Kakahu 63
Te Kotahitanga 22, 51, 98
te reo Māori 32, 37, 50, 51, 59
Te Tapuae o Rehua Ltd 15
teaching as inquiry (TAI) inquiry mindset
- *see also* case study schools; pedagogical changes; priority learners; professional learning and development; school leadership; success stories
- barriers to implementation 48–49, 61–62, 75–77, 121–22
- collaboration between student, teacher and organisation 8, 17
- conditions for successful use 79
- description 1
- Education Review Office (ERO) evaluation 3, 19, 124–25
- focus for inquiry 37–41, 53–55, 65–66, 86–89
- Ministry of Education support for 3
- process 1–4, 5–8, 19–30
- school-wide implementation and development 4, 12, 16, 17, 22, 51, 55, 65, 76, 79, 84, 85, 86, 92, 101–02, 105, 115

sustainability 123–24
teacher intellectual and emotional investments 7–8, 122
teaching resources *see* resource development and use
team processes 29
TEXAS structure for paragraphs 20–21
time factors in TAI 8, 11, 35, 42–43, 44, 48, 66, 75, 78, 109, 118, 127
trust, culture of 28, 30, 61, 98

U
Universal Design for Learning 124
Using research for informing TAI 8, 15, 21, 41, 67, 72, 78, 94, 102, 121
Web 2.0 tools 54
whānau *see* parents and whānau/families
writing skills 20–21, 60, 82, 96, 112
    authentic context 113

www.ingramcontent.com/pod-product-compliance
Lightning Source LLC
Chambersburg PA
CBHW080807300426
44114CB00020B/2860